INVENTORS & INVENTIONS

BIOTECHNOLOGY

INVENTORS & INVENTIONS

BIOTECHNOLOGY

DONNA WELLS

BENCHMARK BOOKS

MARSHALL CAVENDISH

NEW YORK

Benchmark Books
Marshall Cavendish Corporation
99 White Plains Road
Tarrytown, New York 10591-9001

©Marshall Cavendish Corporation, 1996

Series created by The Creative Publishing Company

Library of Congress Cataloging-in-Publication Data

Wells, Donna K.
    Biotechnology / Donna Wells.
        p.   cm. -- (Inventors & inventions)
    Includes index.
    Summary: Describes the history and applications of biotechnology,
focusing on how scientists develop new organisms by altering the
genetic makeup of living things.
    ISBN 0-7614-0046-X
    1. Biotechnology--Juvenile literature.   2. Genetic engineering-
-Juvenile literature.   [1. Biotechnology.   2. Genetic engineering.]
I. Title.   II. Series.
TP248.218.W45   1996
660' .65--dc20   95-30017
                                                                                CIP
                                                                                 AC

Printed in Hong Kong

For Bob, Amy, and Alden

Acknowledgments

Technical Consultant: Steven L. Barnicki, Ph.D.

The publishers would like to thank the following for their permission to reproduce photographs:
Mary Evans Picture Library, (48); King's College, London, (28); Science Photo Library Ltd., (12, James Holmes/ Cellmark Diagnostics cover, Weiss/Jerrican frontispiece, Vanessa Vick 7, Peter Menzel 8, 33, David Parker 9, CNRI 14, Alfred Pasieka 15, Dr. Jeremy Burgess 17, 42, USDA 18, Philippe Plailly/Eurelios 19, 40, 47, 58, World View/Klaas Wertenbroeck 21, J. C. Revy 23, 31, 43, 57, A. Barrington Brown 25, Nancy Kedersha/Immunogen 27, James King-Holmes/ICRF 30, Philippe Plailly 35, Richard T. Nowitz 37, Sinclair Stammers 38, A. B. Dowsett 41, Cindy Charles 44, James King-Holmes 45, 59, Hattie Young 50, Hank Morgan 54, 55); UPI/Bettmann, (11, 13, 16, 46, 53).

(Cover) Preparing the gel used to separate fragments of DNA into bands is the first stage of DNA fingerprinting.

(Frontispiece) A scientist examines genetically engineered seedlings growing in a liquid culture medium.

Contents

— Chapter 1 —
A New Science That's Very Old

Too late! In the last moments before midnight on March 23, 1989, the crew of the oil tanker realized their ship was less than two miles (three kilometers) from the submerged reef. There was little they could do. The shoal, known as Bligh Reef, lay under just thirty feet (nine meters) of water, dangerously close to the shipping channel.

The *Exxon Valdez* had left her Alaskan port earlier that day, laden with oil. She was nearly a thousand feet (three hundred meters) long and just three years old, one of the most technologically advanced ships used in the oil industry. Her hull was full; she carried over a million barrels of oil. By the time crew members recognized the danger they were in, there was no time to turn the ship around.

At precisely 12:04 A.M., the *Exxon Valdez* struck Bligh Reef, tearing long gashes in the bottom of the ship. Crew members watched in horror as oil began pouring out, gliding across the frigid waters of Prince William Sound. By the time it stopped flowing, over ten million gallons (thirty-eight million liters) of oil had escaped. Almost immediately, Alaskan wildlife in and around Prince William Sound began to perish.

It took nearly half a day for researchers and cleanup crews to reach the area of the grounded tanker. First, they tried using long plastic booms to contain the oil. Once the oil was roped off by the booms, the crews hoped to skim the oil off the surface of the water. This technique had been used with smaller spills, but

Eleven thousand people were involved in the attempted cleanup of the Alaskan shoreline after the Exxon Valdez oil spill. Here, workers use high-pressure hot water hoses and pumps to wash the rocks and vacuum the slick away. Eventually, biotechnology provided the best long-term solution to the problem of breaking down the oil.

this time, the spill was simply too big. Soon, vast amounts of oil began washing onto the beaches and the rocky coasts.

Next, cleanup crews tried using *sorbents*, materials that absorb oil. Sorbents can be made from natural materials like straw and sawdust. Others are made from synthetic materials like foam. But again, the *Exxon Valdez* spill was so large that the company quickly ran out of sorbents.

Then, environmentalists suggested a relatively new technique. Why not use oil-eating microbes? Researchers had discovered that microbes would eat the carbon atoms that bond petroleum molecules together. The loss of the carbon would cause the bonds to break, chemically breaking down the fuel. Microbes had been used successfully to clean up fuel-soaked soil in Indiana and Texas.

Ten weeks after the *Exxon Valdez* oil spill, officials from the U.S. Environmental Protection Agency and the oil company decided to try the microbes. First, they placed containers of fertilizer containing the microbes at 750 sites along the shoreline and on the bottom of the sound. In order to stimulate the growth of the bacteria, they spread additional chemical fertilizers. During the next twenty-four months, scientists spread sixteen hundred applications of fertilizer.

It worked! Researchers found that oil broke down five times faster where the munching microbes were used. *Bioremediation*, using the latest available biotechnology to fix an environmental problem, had helped clean up the oil spill.

What Is Biotechnology?

Biotechnology is a technique used by researchers to change life forms in order to develop new or modified organisms. It includes choosing and reproducing the best traits in plants and animals to improve breeds or crops. It also includes changing an inherited characteristic by altering the genetic makeup of a living thing.

The next time you sink your teeth into a juicy, tangy orange, inhale the sweet fragrance of a new variety of rose, or munch on a tomato in the dead of winter, you will be enjoying the benefits of biotechnology. So common are the products of this science that it goes almost unnoticed. It has become an unremarkable part of our everyday lives.

Yet, it is quite remarkable. In fact, it is downright amazing! Without biotechnology, our lives would be very different indeed. We would not be able to produce as much food. We would not be able to domesticate as many animals. And, we would definitely not be able to save as many lives as we can today.

Think for a moment about your typical morning. Your cocker spaniel, Mandy,

A scientist carries out research into producing disease-free potatoes from seed rather than from tubers. Jars of genetically engineered seed, covered with a white protective coating, are on the table. Such improvements would cut potato growers' costs since they normally have to store tons of tubers that often rot before planting.

bounds into your room, jumps on the bed and wakes you up. Over several decades, breeders have been refining purebred dogs like Mandy to produce those with the most desirable characteristics. Without such breeding, Mandy would probably be much smaller, her coat would not be as soft and silky, and her temperament might be very different.

Back to your morning: Still half asleep, you pull on a pair of jeans and a T-shirt. Both are made from cotton. Over the years, farmers and agriculture specialists have developed cotton plants that produce large, soft tufts of cotton. The increased production of improved plants allows you to purchase clothes without worrying about how much cotton is being produced.

Now dressed, you stumble into the kitchen and sit down to breakfast. The grains used to make your cereal result from hybrid plants developed to yield greater quantities of grains that are increasingly resistant to insects and disease. Your cereal is swimming in milk that has been pasteurized, killing bacteria and delaying the souring process. Finally, the orange trees that produced your orange juice were improved to produce plentiful, sweet, juicy fruit.

You have been out of bed less than an hour, and already the science of biotechnology has touched your life in several ways. As you clear your breakfast dishes, you think ahead to lunch. A grilled cheese sandwich sounds great! You can thank biotechnology for the quality of that cheese, too.

A technique called DNA fingerprinting can show how closely related animals are to each other. When one of these Siberian huskies became pregnant, the owner needed to know which dog was the father to establish the puppies' pedigree. Samples of genetic material were taken from the dogs and analyzed, and the problem was solved.

How Long Has Biotechnology Existed?

You may think that biotechnology is a new field of science, but actually it has been around for thousands of years. Ancient people used elementary biotechnology when they learned how to grow wild plants on a plot of land. They found that by gathering the seeds, planting them, and nourishing them, they could produce quantities of food in one place. Early biotechnology also allowed people to tame wild animals. They began to understand that more intelligent animals could be captured, bred, and more easily trained to work. Other animals could be raised as a food source. This meant groups of people no longer had to move from place to place, following the plants or animals they needed to live.

The formal science of biotechnology really began in the mid-nineteenth century. Before that, scientists did not understand inherited traits. Actually at that time, very little was known about how the human body worked. Because blood was one of the most visible parts of the body, many early scientists believed hereditary traits were carried in the blood. Then, along came Gregor Johann Mendel.

Mendel was a poor Austrian peasant born in 1822. He entered the monastery (a place where monks live and study), then became a substitute teacher in a technical school. While there, Mendel began growing and experimenting with garden peas. As he grew them, he collected their seeds to grow the next generation of plants. He found that specific characteristics were passed on from one generation of plant to the next. Tall plants always produced tall plants; flower colors always remained constant among generations. He suggested that "inheritance units" within living organisms always contained certain traits. But he did not know what these inheritance units were.

Between 1856 and 1863, Mendel cultivated thousands of plants, carefully analyzing the seeds and individual characteristics of each. By documenting the behavior of seven characteristics and experimenting in *crossbreeding* (mating individual organisms of different breeds, varieties, or species), Mendel discovered that some traits commonly showed up in successive generations of plants, while other characteristics were masked. Yet even those traits that were masked by the stronger traits still remained in the inheritance units. This led Mendel to define the stronger traits as *dominant* and the weaker traits as *recessive*, terms still used today in the study of genetics.

Mendel's experiments led to the two conclusions that are now called the laws of heredity or Mendel's Laws. They describe how physical characteristics are passed from one generation of plants to the next and how they are inherited as separate units, independent from one another. Mendel published the results of his experiments and his conclusions in 1866, but his work was ignored.

Mendel's Work Is Finally Recognized

It wasn't until thirty-four years later that Mendel's research was once again reviewed and its importance recognized. As so often happens in history, by the turn of the century, several botanists were following separate but parallel paths in their study of individual plant characteristics. A number of them came across the works of Mendel and understood their significance. The most famous of these was a Dutch researcher named Hugo De Vries. The inheritance patterns he observed and recorded were similar to the factors identified by Mendel. He believed that genes, the inheritance units Mendel first described, could be found within cells in rod-shaped structures called *chromosomes*.

Hugo De Vries, like Mendel, worked on the artificial cross-fertilization of plants. In 1901, he noted that some plants had new characteristics he had not expected from his studies of the parent plants. These differences were then inherited by later generations. De Vries gave these new characteristics the name mutations.

Gregor Johann Mendel (1822–1884)

Johann Mendel was born into a peasant family in a small Moravian village in the country now known as the Czech Republic. As a child, he attended the village elementary school where studies included classes in science. Fortunately, he enjoyed school so much that his family allowed him to attend a more advanced school in a neighboring town. But when he was sixteen years old, his father had a serious accident, and the family was forced to sell the little land they owned. Lacking money for additional educational opportunities, having few social connections and little professional preparation, Mendel entered an Austrian monastery at Brünn (now Brno, in the Czech Republic). He was accepted as a novice in 1843, taking the Christian name Gregor.

The monastery was a fortunate choice. At the time, Brünn was the capital of Moravia, and the monastery had built a strong reputation as a regional center of scientific study and learning. Mendel enjoyed his studies of theology but also continued his love of biology.

In 1849, Mendel was appointed to a teaching position at a high school in southern Moravia. Because his formal education was incomplete, his religious order sent him to the University of Vienna to complete his studies. It was during his early teaching career that his lifelong interest in science led him to begin experimenting with mice, attempting to understand the mysteries of heredity. But at some point, his experiments changed direction.

Although historians are unsure why Mendel stopped using mice, they do know that he chose the garden pea with extreme care and forethought. He had initially tried other types of plants, but each had its own problems. The garden pea, on the other hand, had several advantages. First, Mendel had access to varieties that had been carefully cultivated over several years. Second, the peas possessed pairs of characteristics, such as height and flower color, that were more easily studied than mice traits. Finally, the plant was relatively easy to grow and maintain.

Mendel's first step was to pollinate each of the plants himself, making sure none of them could be accidentally pollinated by insects. He wanted to be certain that any inherited traits could be traced back to a single parent plant. Once he was sure that parent plants always produced offspring with similar traits, he began cross-pollinating plants to see what would happen to the characteristics.

Until this time, scientists believed that crossbred plants would produce blended traits. For example, if a tall plant were crossbred with a dwarf plant, scientists concluded the offspring would be of medium height. Instead, Mendel proved that traits were not blended but rather that characteristics were passed on intact.

No one knows exactly why, in the 1870s, he stopped his scientific experiments. He may have become discouraged by the comments he received from other scientists. We do know that in 1868, Mendel became abbot (head) of the monastery. His duties there probably became very time consuming. However, over the years, Mendel was also consuming greater and greater amounts of food (we know he wasn't eating his peas!). He grew quite large. Eventually, it may have become difficult for him to move around among his plants. Fortunately, by the time he gave up his experiments, his most critical work had been completed.

Mendel lived the rest of his life in the monastery at Brünn. He died there on January 6, 1884, when he was sixty-one years old. Today, he is recognized as the father of genetics.

Gregor Mendel carries out experiments in his monastery garden.

De Vries was also the first scientist to report mutations of inherited traits. Mutations are sudden changes in the genes or chromosomes that cause different characteristics in the offspring than found in the parents. They are most often recessive traits and are usually considered harmful to an organism.

In 1868, quite by accident, another important discovery in genetics was made. Johan Friedrich Miescher, a Swiss biochemist, had been trying to prove that cells were composed of protein. Although Miescher was able to break down the cell and identify its makeup, he couldn't break down the cell nucleus. Instead, he found that the nucleus contained an unusual substance very different from other materials in the cell. He called this substance "nuclein."

Miescher had no idea of the importance of his discovery, but he had, in fact, discovered nucleic acid. This was the first time anyone had identified the chemical family to which DNA (deoxyribonucleic acid, the chemical that contains all the genes of an organism) belongs.

The Structure of Cells

The typical cell has a nucleus that controls all the cell's major functions. Spread throughout the nucleus are strands of chromosomes. Some organisms, such as bacteria, have only one chromosome. Usually, the more complex an organism is, the more chromosomes it has. Chromosomes all contain a nucleic acid, usually DNA.

The nucleus is separated from the rest of the cell by the nuclear membrane. This membrane is porous; it allows some materials to pass from the nucleus to the

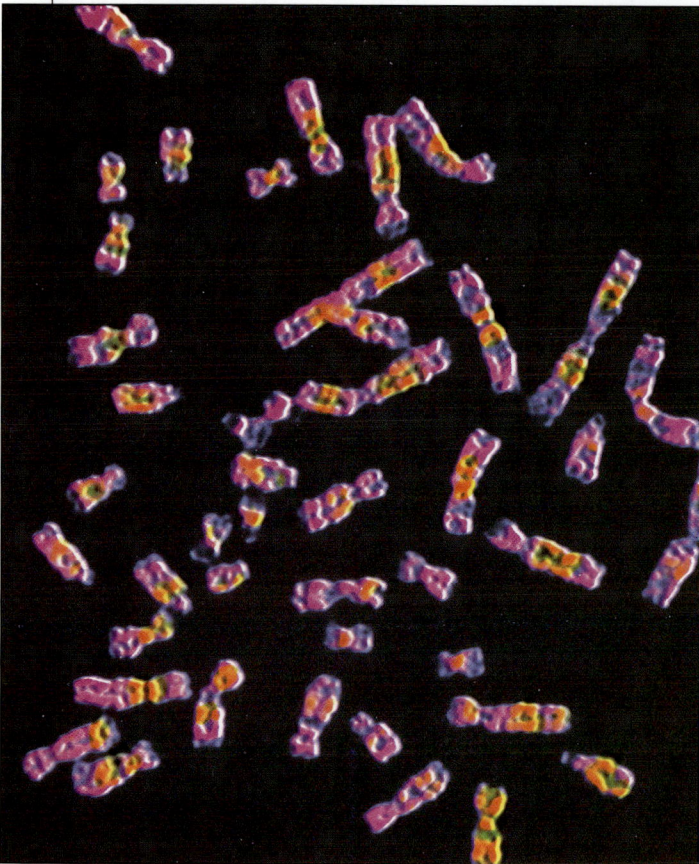

A false-color image of human chromosomes. These are threadlike structures in a cell's nucleus that carry genetic information. The nucleus of every human cell contains forty-six chromosomes, twenty-three from each parent. Chromosomes can construct exact copies of themselves. So, when a cell divides into two, both new cells have the same chromosomes.

surrounding jellylike material called *cytoplasm*. Cytoplasm, found in all cells, contains several structures that help direct the cell's activities.

Because the cell is simply a collection of chemical compounds, it must be held together and protected. This is the function of the cell membrane, a thin coating that surrounds the cell while allowing nutrients to pass into it and waste materials to pass out.

The Importance of DNA

In 1906, an English biologist, William Bateson, first used the word *genetics* to describe how physical and behavioral traits are passed from parents to their offspring. At about the same time, across the Atlantic in the United States, Thomas Hunt Morgan, a scientist at Columbia University, used Mendel's basic experiment to test the hereditary characteristics of fruit flies. Through his research, he determined that hereditary traits are lined up along the chromosomes. These rod-shaped bodies may be small, but their job isn't. They contain all the inheritance information for the cell. This discovery was so important that Morgan eventually won the Nobel Prize for his research.

A cross-section of a human cell shows the nucleus as a large oval in the center. Humans are made up of billions of cells, while, at the other extreme, bacteria are single-cell organisms.

In 1944, scientists Oswald T. Avery, Colin M. MacLeod, and Maclyn McCarty replaced a defective gene in a microorganism called a bacterium with DNA from another bacterium. Their success at transferring a healthy gene helped prove that DNA is the key to genetic traits. This knowledge has allowed scientists to deliberately change living organisms through genetic engineering.

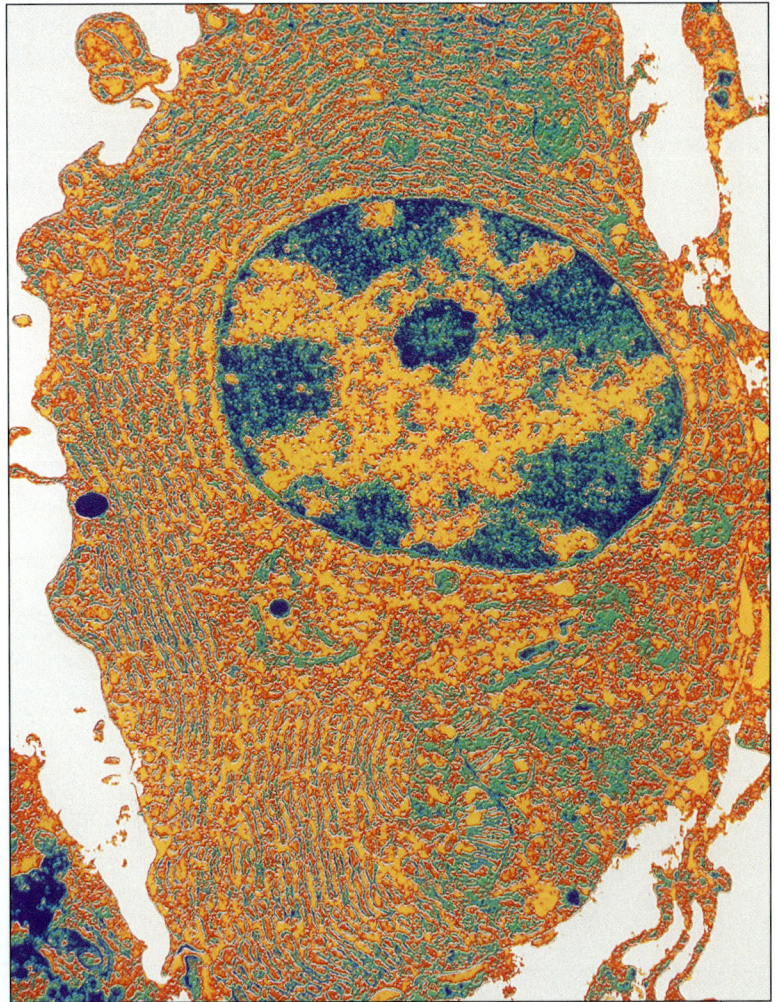

15

Thomas Hunt Morgan (1866–1945)

Several of the earliest biotechnical discoveries occurred almost by accident. In the early 1900s, when Thomas Hunt Morgan was experimenting with the fruit fly at Columbia University, he noticed that one of his male specimens had white eyes instead of red, the normal color for fruit flies. This observation eventually led to an amazing discovery.

Morgan was an American biologist born in Lexington, Kentucky, on September 25, 1866. He spent his early years at home, then was accepted at State College of Kentucky. When he graduated, he began studying *embryology*, the study of how organisms develop, at Johns Hopkins University. He earned his Ph.D. in 1891 and took a position teaching experimental zoology at Columbia University.

Morgan began his work, basing his experiments on Mendel's theories but substituting fruit flies for the garden peas. He chose to use fruit flies because they were easy to raise and they reproduced very quickly.

Morgan took his white-eyed male fruit fly and bred it with a red-eyed female. Every offspring was born with the normal red eyes. In the second generation of offspring, however, some of the flies had white eyes. Oddly enough, all of the white-eyed flies were males. In succeeding generations, while most offspring had red eyes, occasionally a white-eyed fly would appear. Nearly all the white-eyed offspring were male, although sometimes a white-eyed female would be produced. Because of this, Morgan decided that some traits are sex-linked.

Thomas Hunt Morgan signs autographs after being awarded the Nobel Prize in 1933.

Like other traits, the sex of an organism is determined by its chromosomes. Every human being, for example, has twenty-three pairs of chromosomes in each cell. The only difference in the chromosomes of men and women is found in the twenty-third pair. In females, the twenty-third pair is made up of two chromosomes, each shaped like an X. They are called X chromosomes. But in males, the twenty-third pair is made up of an X chromosome and another chromosome shaped more like a Y. It is known as the Y (or male) chromosome.

Morgan decided that the fruit fly gene for white eyes is located on the X (female) chromosome in each organism. Because white eyes are a recessive trait, a female fly would have to inherit two white-eye genes on her X chromosomes to have white eyes. Otherwise the more common red-eye gene would dominate. But if a male inherited an X chromosome containing the white-eye trait, he would have no other X chromosome to dominate it, so his eyes would be white. And males would exhibit the trait more frequently because the X chromosome would be paired with a Y chromosome, not another X chromosome.

Morgan's laboratory at Columbia University eventually became known as the "fly room." He published his results of his fruit fly studies in *The Mechanism of Mendelian Heredity* in 1915. It is now simply called the chromosome theory. In 1926, Morgan also published *The Theory of the Gene*, suggesting that genes cluster together in groups and that pairs of genes can cross over one another in the same linkage group.

Unlike Mendel, Morgan's work was recognized during his lifetime. He won the Nobel Prize in 1933 and died just twelve years later in Pasadena, California.

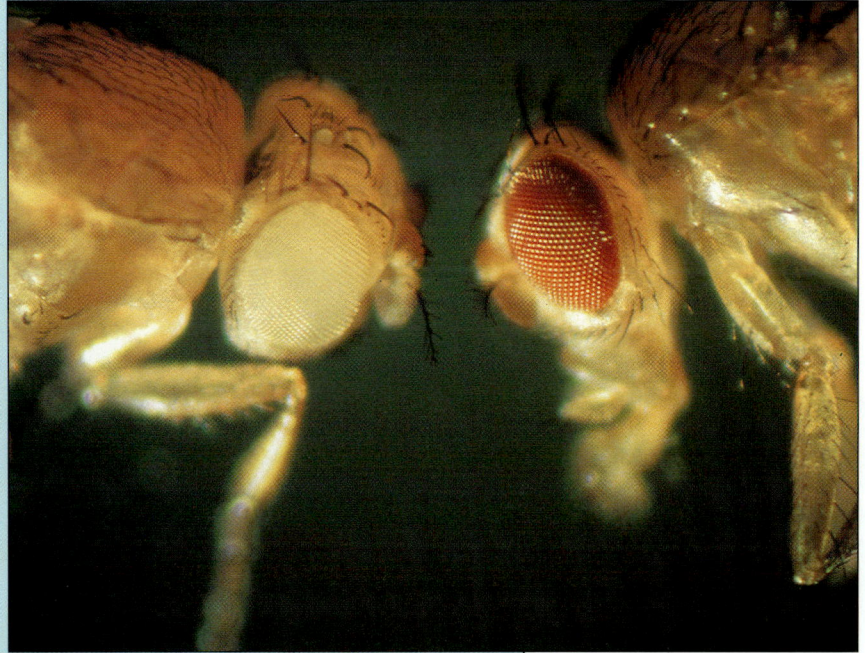

A normal fruit fly (right) with red eyes and the mutant white-eyed form (left). Fruit flies are still used by scientists for genetic studies.

Experimental plants are often grown in test tubes, suspended in a growth medium. They are genetically selected for maximum growth and productivity so they often have all been propagated from one mother plant, making them genetically identical.

AMAZING FACTS

In May 1995, scientists received approval to produce a potato that has a pesticide implanted in it. Called the NewLeaf potato, but humorously dubbed "Darth Tater," the potato includes a gene (transferred from a bacterium) that kills the Colorado potato beetle. The beetle-killing gene's toxin is not harmful to humans or animals, but it will likely prove fatal to a number of insects. Researchers believe they need just two or three more years of experimentation to learn if there are any unwanted consequences to the new potato, but right now, they believe the NewLeaf will eventually be on store shelves throughout the United States.

The Two Sides of Biotechnology

Yet, not all scientific work in biotechnology results in positive changes. For example, the dog breeders who selectively breed cocker spaniels like Mandy are more interested in how those dogs look than in what they can do. Hundreds of years ago, spaniels were working dogs. They were strong swimmers and helped their owners hunt. But breeders today want dogs with more beautiful coats, more perfect bone structures, and more show-winning personalities. Unfortunately, while such dogs are beautiful to look at, many have lost the traits that once made them such helpful workers.

In the hundred and fifty years since Mendel conducted his experiments with pea plants, the study of genetics and how to engineer changes in genes has grown by leaps and bounds. It continues to change, sometimes on a daily basis, as scientists strive to understand the gene — our basic unit of heredity.

Chapter 2
The Evolution of Genetics

Diverse may be the best word to describe our world. Thousands upon thousands of organisms exist here. They range from the smallest microscopic single-celled animals to the largest of mammals. Even within one organism, different types of cells behave very differently.

As a new organism develops, one of the most incredible and complex of all functions is the way that cells begin to take on special tasks. As a fertilized cell grows, divides, and divides again, it becomes a large mass of cells. Each new cell that is created

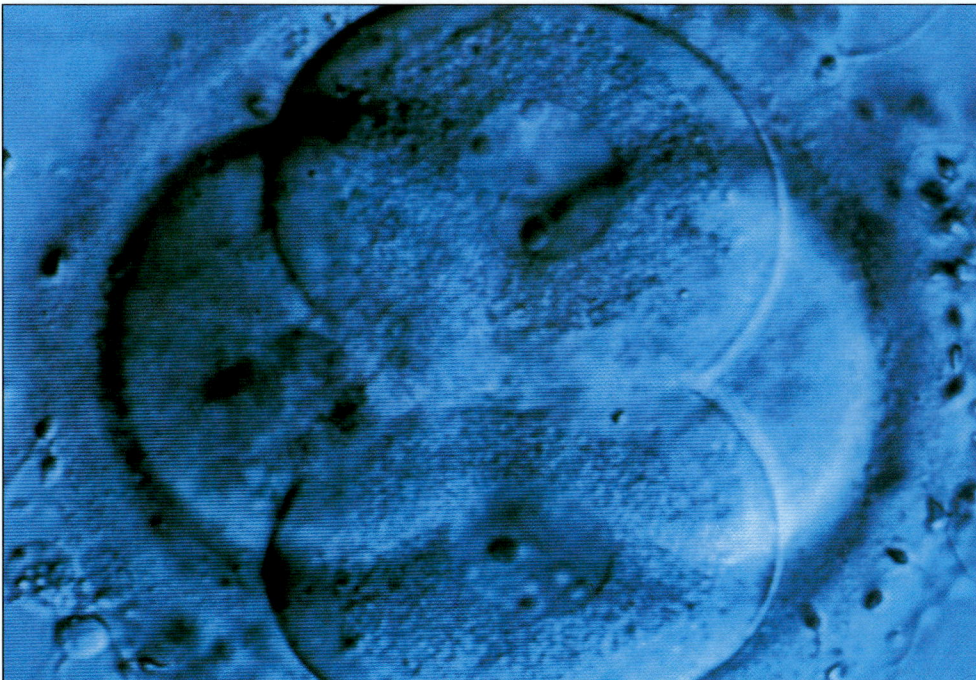

A human embryo begins to form. At this stage, it is composed of only four cells, the result of a single cell splitting twice in two. A central nucleus can be seen in each cell. The embryo will continue to divide and grow, eventually implanting in the mother's womb.

carries an entire set of genetic instructions. This means that every cell in your body contains the information needed to produce another being exactly like you.

At some point, after a fertilized egg has divided many times, cell differentiation takes place; the cells begin to specialize according to certain functions. One type of cell becomes muscle tissue. Another group of cells becomes part of the bone structure. Still another becomes part of the heart and another part of the intestine. Researchers do not understand exactly how this takes place, but they think that cells contain an *activator-repressor* mechanism that acts like a control switch, turning genes on and off at certain times. This switch controls development so that an eye will contain all of its proper parts and a foot will have five toes and be correctly located at the end of a leg.

The Discovery of DNA's Structure

Although the structure of the cell was first described by Robert Hooke in 1665, scientists did not understand how cells could reproduce copies of themselves. They couldn't figure out exactly how inherited traits could be developed in every new cell. It took nearly three hundred years to solve this mystery. Yet once researchers understood Mendel's studies, a new scientific window opened, and scientists throughout Europe and the United States began focusing on microbiology and gene research.

In 1953, two young researchers, Francis Crick and James D. Watson, published a short scientific paper that shook the scientific world. Watson and Crick had discovered the structure of DNA. They determined that it is made up of two strands of material twisted into a double helix shape (similar to a twisted spiral ladder). Sugar and phosphate groups form the long strands (side rails) of the ladder. Four nitrogen bases — adenine (A), thymine (T), guanine (G), and cytosine (C) — attached to the sugars, and linked up with each other to form base pairs (adenine with thymine, and cytosine with guanine), make up the steps of the

---

AMAZING FACTS

Even though every human being begins life as a single cell, by the time a person is an adult, he or she has about fifty trillion (50,000,000,000,000) cells! The single cell divides in two, then divides again. Soon there is a growing mass of cells. It takes less than fifty divisions for that single cell to become trillions of cells!

(Opposite) A computer graphics representation of a section of DNA. The double helix is like a twisted ladder with complementary pairs of organic bases [adenine (A) and thymine (T), cytosine (C) and guanine (G)] as its rungs. The order of these bases encodes genetic information. Sequences of them instruct cells how to form proteins.

ladder. The amount of each base is different in different organisms. Humans have greater amounts of A and T. Other animals possess more C and G. Some organisms have nearly equal amounts of both. The way the bases are lined up determines hereditary traits. A single gene may have hundreds of bases.

When a new organism is developing, its cells have to divide. This means that every gene in the cell must produce an exact copy of itself. When cell division is needed, the DNA strands inside the cell begin to unwind and separate. Every C separates from its complementary G. Each A pulls apart from its companion T. The cell also contains free-floating chemicals called nucleotides. Some of these nucleotides join each separated strand of the spiral, and two new ladders are formed from the original one.

Because the chemicals always pair up in exactly the same way, the DNA almost always makes an identical copy of itself. Once the copy is made, the cell can divide, and the complete instructions for the organism will be found in both cells.

So important was the discovery of the DNA structure, that Crick called it the "secret of life." While some researchers might disagree, Crick

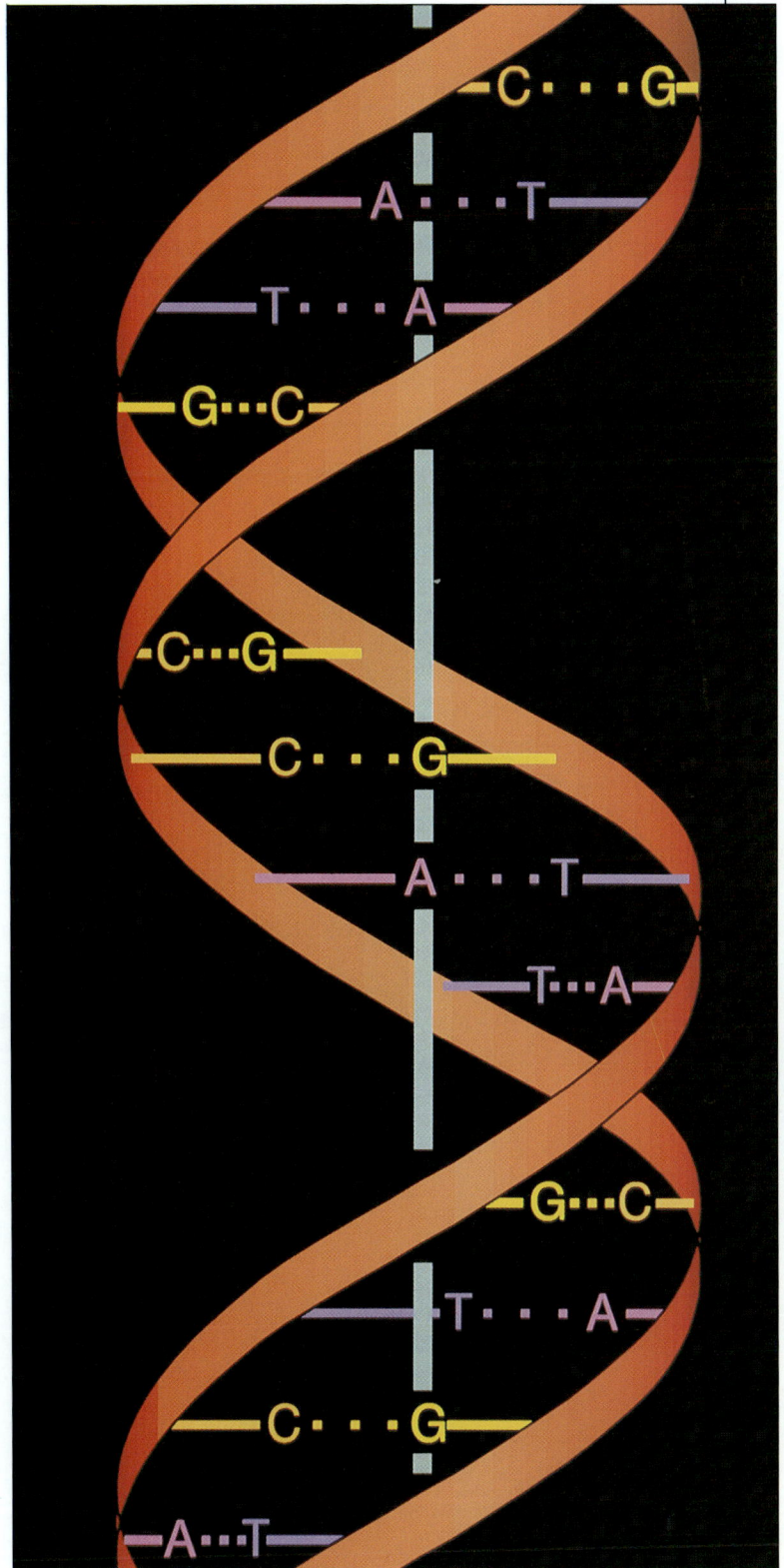

and Watson's discovery has provided the basis for modern biotechnology. No longer do we have to use whole organisms to develop new ones. Now, a single gene, carrying one trait, can be taken from one organism and inserted in another.

Can Errors Occur in the Genetic Code?

When builders construct a new building, they must follow the blueprint developed by the architect. The foundation must be strong enough to support the weight of the building. The walls must be placed in a certain pattern to bear the load of the structure and to divide the building into rooms. The wiring and plumbing must be of the right kind and must be placed in correct locations. Building construction is a complex process that must be completed in a certain order, according to a detailed blueprint.

Like construction, the reproduction of DNA is a very precise process. Unfortunately, it does not always work as it should. On occasion, during the replication phase, a segment of DNA ends up with the wrong information. This can cause a mutation or abnormality. Abnormalities can also occur if an entire gene is missing or if an extra gene forms.

Your Genes Are History!

Less than fifty years ago, scientists weren't even sure exactly how hereditary information was stored in cells. Once Watson and Crick figured out the structure of DNA, the genetic code was broken. We now understand that DNA controls everything we do. In fact, it controls everything that is done by all living organisms. The more we learn about DNA, the more we will understand ourselves and all other living creatures.

Think about your own set of genes. They go back a long way! You inherited half of them from each parent. One quarter of your genetic makeup was contributed by each of your grandparents and one eighth by each of your great-grandparents. You also

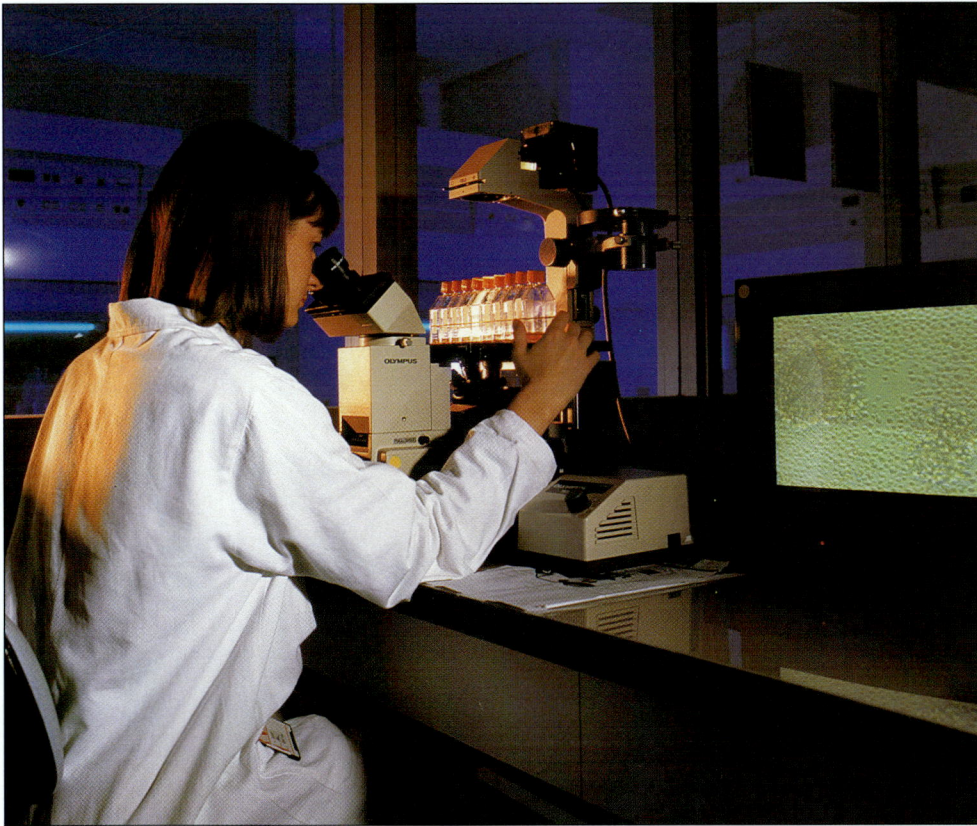

A researcher examines a cell culture from a patient with an inherited disease in order to find the fragments of DNA that cause the disease. Eventually, all human DNA will be mapped, allowing scientists to pinpoint the genes responsible for all hereditary disorders.

share a quarter of your gene pool with any blood-related aunt or uncle. Unless you are an identical twin, no one else has exactly the same genetic makeup as you. Identical twins have identical genetic codes because they develop from a single fertilized egg.

We know that both heredity and the environment are critical to our health and well-being, yet we still do not know for certain how much the environment influences our development. With continued advances in biotechnology, that distinction may become even more blurred. For example, scientists now believe that an individual's weight may be related to a specific gene. However, if a person has a genetic tendency to gain weight and lives in a society that produces lots of fatty foods, then the individual's weight gain may be caused by a combination of inherited traits and environmental factors. Heredity or environment? In the end, the question may not be which is more important, but rather, how much influence do they have over each other, and thus, over us?

AMAZING FACTS

Why do older people have so many health problems? Do older animals or older plants also suffer from age-related difficulties? Researchers are trying to determine whether an individual's genetic code deteriorates as the individual grows older. Some scientists believe that such deterioration could lead to some of the problems associated with old age.

23

Francis Harry Compton Crick and James Dewey Watson

The team of Francis Harry Compton Crick and James Dewey Watson, credited with discovering the structure of DNA, was aided in their search by a series of coincidences, unusual timing, and sheer luck. Yet in the end, they were the first to illustrate the structure of DNA.

Francis Crick was born in Northampton, England, in 1916. By most accounts, he did not show any early interest in science. As a young adult, however, he did pursue studies in physics. He earned a degree from University College in London in 1938, then began research that he hoped would lead to a doctorate.

Unfortunately, World War II broke out, interrupting his studies. For the next seven years, beginning in 1940, Crick worked on the development of radar. Eventually, he was able to complete his Ph.D. in physics from Caius College, University of Cambridge in England. Coincidentally, during this time, he heard Linus Pauling, a famous American chemist, give a presentation on the practice of using physics to attack biological problems. Increasingly, Crick became less interested in pure physics and more interested in applying it to problems of living organisms. In 1949, this new direction led him to join the Laboratory of Molecular Biology at Cambridge.

Meanwhile, twelve years after the birth of Crick and a continent away, James D. Watson was born in Chicago, Illinois. Unlike Crick, Watson took an early and intense interest in biology. In 1943, at age fifteen, he was accepted into an experimental program at the University of Chicago and encouraged to study zoology. Four years later, he graduated, then enrolled in the doctoral program at Indiana University where he earned his Ph.D. in 1950.

The following year, Watson attended a meeting in Italy where he learned that x-ray studies of DNA were being conducted. Realizing the significance of the work, Watson decided to move to Cambridge to join the team of scientists there working on molecular biology. It was then that the paths of Watson and Crick first crossed.

From 1951 to 1953, the two conducted research together at Cambridge. They based their work on previous studies done by another scientist, Maurice Wilkins.

Using this and other chemical knowledge, in January 1953, Watson and Crick began building proposed models of DNA. Less than two months later, using metal plates from a machine shop, the two constructed the first accurate model of the double helix. Their model of DNA was completed on March 7, 1953. Two days later, Crick received word that Maurice Wilkins, working in the laboratory at King's College, was also close to providing a model of the structure. By March 18, Watson and Crick had drafted and circulated through Cambridge the paper describing the discovery.

Their model, which they first published in the April 1953 issue of *Nature*, explained exactly how hereditary information is copied and passed on. It also explained how you are able to act like your mother or look like your father. Watson and Crick had raced to beat other scientists working on the same problem and so will go down in history for the discovery of the structure of DNA. In 1962, along with Wilkins, Crick and Watson won the Nobel Prize in the category of "physiology or medicine."

Afterward, Crick moved on to study how organisms develop. He was searching for the key to unlock the mystery of how cells take on special functions, hoping to learn why some cells become brain cells while others become muscle cells. Eventually, Crick took a professorship at the Salk Institute and focused his work on nerve cells.

Watson, on the other hand, spent the next fifteen years at Harvard University as a biology professor, then turned his attention to the study of cancer. In 1968, he published *The Double Helix*, describing the DNA discovery. He went on to become the first director of the Human Genome Project (*see* Chapter 7).

James Watson (left) and Francis Crick with their model of DNA in 1953.

Chapter 3
Traveling the Genetic Highway

We still have so much to learn about the human body. Often, when scientists think they know the answer to a question, something forces them to question their own conclusions. If left unchecked, cancer, for example, continues to thrive in the human body until it is removed or destroyed. At least that is what normally happens. But, Tommy Cram, a teenager from Centreville, Virginia, is causing doctors to question once again whether deadly cancers can just disappear. And, if so, how?

In 1994, Tommy was diagnosed with brain cancer. He immediately had surgery to remove the tumor, but in December, doctors found that the cancer had spread to his spine. They told Tommy's parents there was no hope he would survive.

The family decided to try a new treatment at Duke University Medical Center in North Carolina, but the procedure made Tommy ill, so he asked the doctors to stop. Then he went home and made his plans to die.

Still, Tommy returned periodically to the doctors for monitoring, and much to everyone's surprise, a brain scan in April 1995 showed that Tommy's cancer was in remission. The family was afraid to believe it, so they had more extensive testing done in May. The results were even more dramatic. The cancer had disappeared.

Neither the family nor the doctors can explain how it happened. Is there a genetic answer that will tell us why some people survive deadly diseases while others do not? If so, doctors want to find it and study it. Someday, it may provide the clue researchers need to find cures for our most harmful illnesses.

Creeping Along at a Snail's Pace

Each cell in the human body has twenty-three pairs of chromosomes. The DNA in each chromosome is riddled with genes. Scientists realize that in order to use genetics to prevent certain diseases or disorders, they first must locate the correct genes within the chromosome. This task is especially difficult because there are so many chromosomes and also because, in the past, it took such a long time to record and analyze genetic changes. Scientists estimate that the human body possesses between fifty thousand and one hundred thousand genes. Locating and mapping all of them seems like a very slow laborious process. And initially, it was.

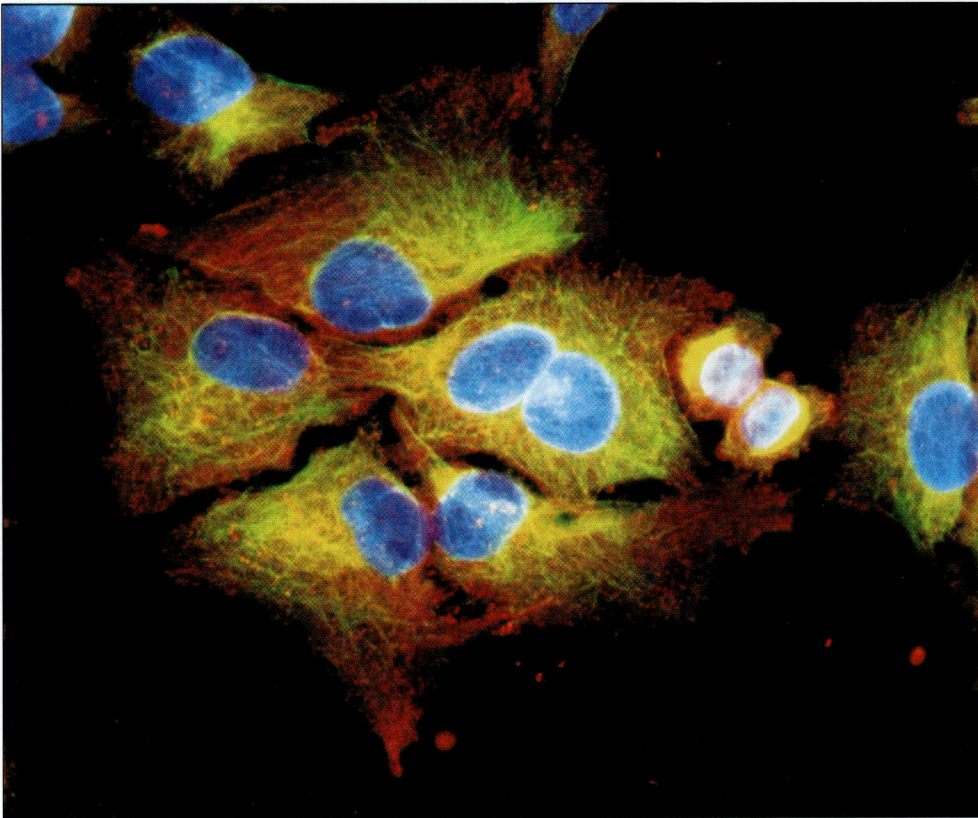

AMAZING FACTS

The best example of the replication of abnormal cells may be the cancer cells taken from a woman known as Helen Lane (not her real name). In 1951, doctors removed the cells from her diseased cervix. That family of cells continued to grow and divide and has been used by researchers around the world in countless experiments. They are known as the HeLa strain of cells.

A culture of HeLa cells, the nuclei colored blue with fluorescent dye. -At center right, a cell is dividing.

27

Rosalind Elsie Franklin (1920–1958)

The race to discover the structure of DNA was so close that, except for a couple of unusual coincidences, the outcome might have been very different. The one person who played a significant role in assisting all the teams working on the project was Rosalind Franklin.

Franklin was born in London in 1920. She earned her degree in physical chemistry from Cambridge, then began working in France. But family matters forced Franklin to return to England in 1951.

She had become an expert in using x-rays to study the structure of materials, so she was quickly hired by the team working on DNA at King's College. King's College in London was the first institution in Britain to establish a biophysics lab. Although the unit had been started by John Randall, one of its primary members was Maurice Wilkins.

Wilkins had been working on the development of the atomic bomb but had become discouraged and decided to turn to the study of the structure of living organisms. He chose to embark on x-ray studies of DNA in hopes of finding the key that would unlock the mystery of its structure. At the time Franklin was hired at King's College, there was some indication that Wilkins had turned his attention away from DNA research. Apparently, that was not the case.

Perhaps that was the first twist of fate that spelled failure for the King's College team. Franklin

believed she had been employed to head up the DNA studies. But, upon her arrival, she learned instead that Maurice Wilkins would do so and that she, in fact, was to be a junior member of the team. The misunderstanding did nothing to enhance the working relationship between Wilkins and Franklin. Still, Franklin chose to stay at King's and join the research team.

Her first task was to set up an x-ray diffraction laboratory at the college. That effort alone took eight precious months, time that was used by Watson and Crick to further their studies of DNA's structure. Once the lab was established, she began working to decipher DNA's shape. In November 1951, Franklin delivered her first research paper in which she suggested that the DNA structure was a helix.

Unfortunately, at some point over the next few months, Franklin apparently abandoned the idea that DNA was a helix-shaped structure and began evaluating other possible forms. Again, this was a mistake that proved valuable to the timing of Watson and Crick. Events were moving so quickly that all the teams working on the problem seemed to be rushing toward the same end in a sort of scientific free-for-all. The structure of DNA was about to be discovered by someone. And at least three of the teams appeared to be running neck-in-neck.

By December 1952, the breakthrough was within reach of all the teams, including scientists working in the United States. It was at that point that Watson made a fateful visit to London. During a meeting and without Franklin's permission, Wilkins gave Watson one of Franklin's photographs of DNA. Not only did that break all the rules of research, it proved to be the clue that Watson and Crick needed. The print showed them that the DNA structure could logically be a double helix. As soon as Watson returned to Cambridge, they began building the model that turned out to be the correct one.

Franklin, meanwhile, had decided to leave King's College. She moved to Birkbeck College where she hoped to find a less stressful environment. In the DNA race, she had been close, but not close enough. Even though she held much promise as a researcher, unfortunately, Franklin died from cancer just five years after the discovery of the structure of DNA and four years before the Nobel Prize was awarded for the discovery.

Although great strides were being made in genetic research, in the first thirty years after Watson and Crick discovered the structure of DNA, only a few genes had actually been located. One way researchers mapped genes was to study inheritance patterns in families. Typically, genes that are located close together are inherited together more often than genes located farther apart. By studying family histories, researchers tried to identify genes that keep reoccurring in family members with genetic diseases.

Scientists eventually learned to use genetic "markers" (pieces of DNA that are inherited along with genes) as guideposts in their mapping. Markers act like street signs along the way. Typically, such signposts may occur five million bases apart (a distance far too small to be seen with the naked eye). Even when researchers successfully use markers to find the general location of a gene, they still must search through thousands of genes to pinpoint the exact location of the particular gene they need.

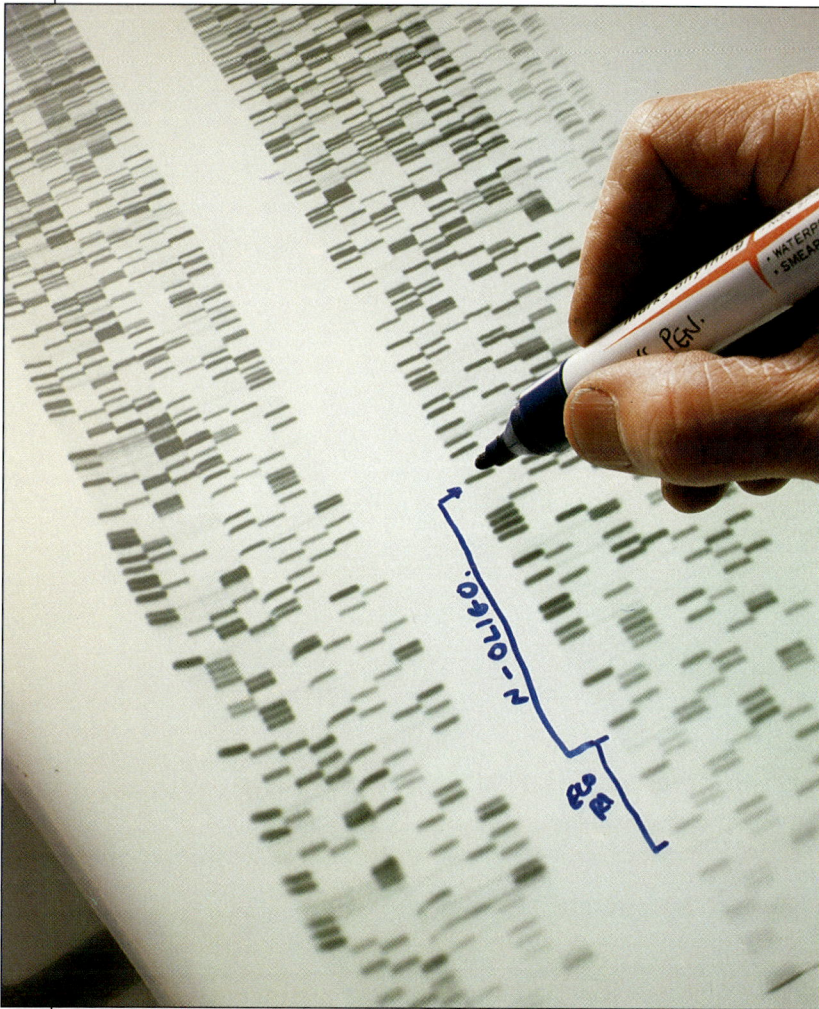

The structure of DNA is analyzed. A technique called gel electrophoresis *separates fragments of DNA into bands according to size. These black bands reveal gene sequences. A single gene can extend over many bands. Although certain regions of DNA are unique to each individual, more than 99 percent of DNA is identical in all humans.*

From Crawling to "Walking" to "Jumping"

By 1985, scientists had discovered a way to "walk" along a strand of DNA using certain proteins to snip apart pieces of DNA on a chromosome. Then, scientists would group related pieces of DNA together. Using this method, scientists could work their way along the DNA segments, using landmarks and studying the bases as they walked. Although the process works, it is very slow.

At the University of Michigan, Francis S. Collins developed a shortcut known as "jumping." Jumping lets researchers scan across large segments of DNA without examining all of the information in the middle. It reduces the time needed to find a particular gene.

In 1985, researcher Lap-Chee Tsui was looking for the gene responsible for cystic fibrosis. Cystic fibrosis is an inherited disease that kills those infected with it. In his search for the gene that causes cystic fibrosis, Tsui began walking along segments of DNA. But the process was slow, so he teamed up with Francis Collins. Together, they used jumping to locate the gene. It took

Gene banks store cells in liquid nitrogen at a temperature of minus 196 degrees Celsius. Each of the test tubes seen here contains about one million cells, all from patients affected by genetic diseases. Scientist are trying to find timesaving ways of analyzing all this stored information.

just four years. Tsui said that if he had "walked" the segment of DNA, it would have taken him eighteen years to locate the gene.

So Much to Do, so Little Time

In the last ten years, there have been many changes in the way researchers find, unlock, and copy genetic material. That's why breakthroughs in technology are important. Each new invention increases the speed at which genes can be identified, located, and copied.

In 1985, the Cetus Corporation developed a procedure that aids genetic research. Scientists there found a way to copy a segment of DNA millions of times over. The process is known as *polymerase chain reaction* (PCR). By using it, millions of copies of DNA material can be made from a tiny drop of blood. The most common use of this technique now is in criminal investigations when human material such as blood or a strand of hair is part of the evidence in the case. Like fingerprints, each person's DNA structure is unique. This allows law enforcement officers and forensic specialists to match a suspect's DNA sample with DNA evidence left at the crime scene. Being able to produce copies of DNA material gives them sufficient samples to use in their investigations.

Our Past and Our Future

Has anyone ever told you how much you resemble your mother? Or that you act just like your father did when he was your age? Have you ever wondered what parts of your personality you inherited? Or is your personality formed by events that happened to you years ago?

Early scientists searched to find out how traits were carried from one generation to the next. Today, researchers are looking at how to use those traits to direct our future. Now that they've unlocked the secrets of DNA, they are using their knowledge to improve our health, our environment, and our well-being.

— Chapter 4 —
Altering Genetic Makeup

Genetically identical grape vines are mass-produced by cloning from tiny fragments, or even single cells, of one parent plant.

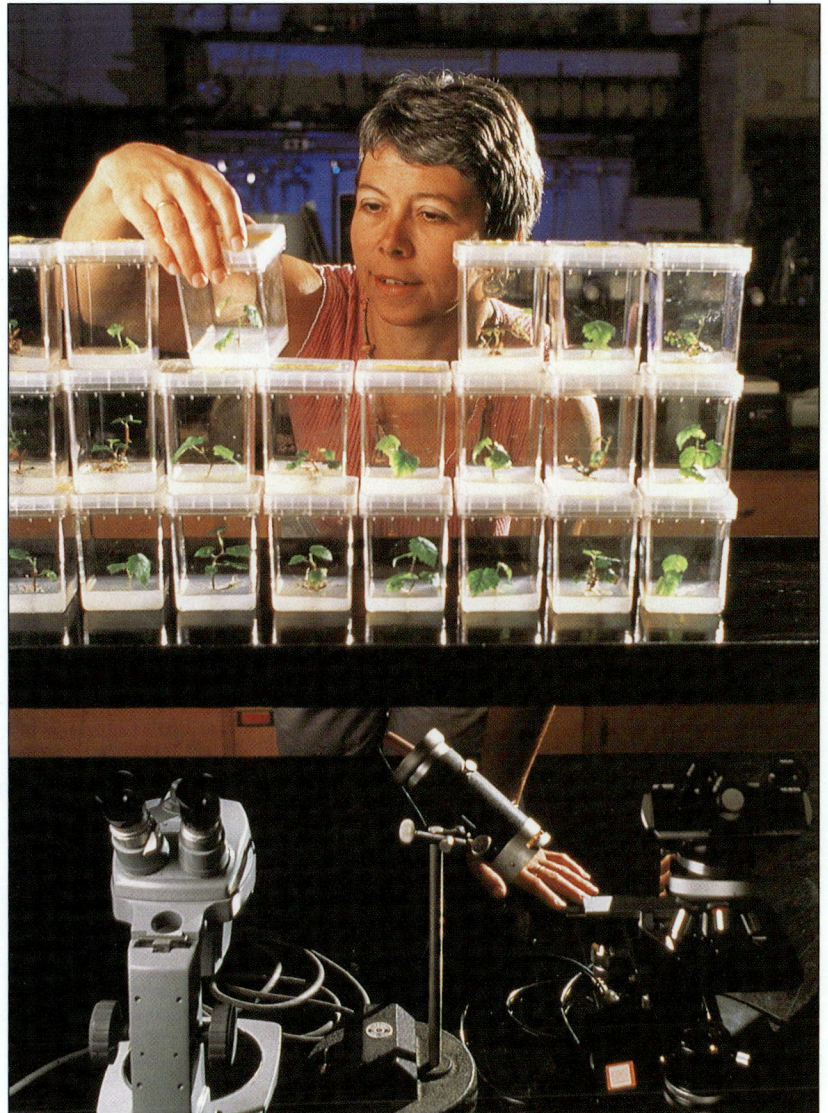

For millions of years, our world has maintained a natural order. Some organisms, such as the dinosaur, have become extinct. Others have evolved to meet changes in the environment. A plant or animal is usually kept in check in its own environment by natural predators. This process maintains a delicate ecological balance.

Interestingly, nature does have its own forms of natural genetic alteration. For years, one example puzzled scientists. Countless gardeners had noticed that sometimes plants growing in very wet soil would be wounded in some way and then would develop a gall (rounded lump) at the site of the wound. The gall could infest a large variety of plants, but it was not fatal. Instead, it turned out to be a perfect example of natural genetic engineering.

The crown gall bacterium lives in the soil. It has the ability to insert its DNA material directly into a wounded plant's cell structure through the wound. The altered cells of the wounded plant then begin growing and producing nutrients for the bacterium. In this way, the bacterium is able to live without destroying its host plant. This natural genetic transfer offered a model for researchers as they experimented with gene transfer.

Artificial Genetic Engineering

How does nature transfer genetic information from one organism to another? Every time a bee transports pollen from one plant to another, hereditary information is being transmitted. But this transfer is random and natural.

In contrast, when scientists transfer genetic material from one organism to another, that genetic transfer is neither random nor natural. Instead, it is deliberate and controlled. Multiply the number of genes stored in each type of organism on earth by the number of gene transfers potentially available, and the possible outcomes are almost beyond imagination. But every day, scientists are imagining and experimenting with different types of genetic engineering in order to improve the way we live.

Still, these improvements may come with unwanted side effects. Even though we have been experimenting with the gene structure of plants, we don't yet fully understand it. That makes such experimentation risky — we are creating new organisms without knowing exactly what they will be.

Some genetic researchers argue that our ecosystem has always been able to respond to and control newly evolved species. But natural evolutions occur slowly over time and usually in small isolated environments.

Genetic engineering, in contrast, has the potential to introduce large numbers of organisms into an ecosystem in a very short time. And we may not know all of the consequences of this until after it is too late.

Disease-Resistant Crops

Yet the field of biotechnology is exploding with new information. One of the greatest agricultural challenges for scientists is to improve the crops we grow for our food. Some plants produce natural insecticides that help them resist attacks from insects. Researchers are experimenting with these plants, hoping that similar genes can be introduced into other crops to increase their resistance to insects.

A lettuce with sterile male parts is artificially pollinated from a fertile male plant that has been genetically altered to be resistant to a herbicide. This prevents the passing of nonresistant genes to future generations of the plant.

Again, there is a risk to these experiments because we don't know how they will affect the rest of the ecosystem. For example, if we develop a new crop that is more resistant to disease, we may not be able to control its growth. It could change, forever, the ecological balance of its environment.

As each new organism is created, scientists must weigh the risks against the benefits the new organism may provide. This is even more necessary when scientists begin exchanging genes between plants and animals. The arctic flounder, for example, can grow and live in near-freezing waters because of a genetic trait. Researchers have begun to study whether such a gene might be used to protect citrus and other fruits from frost damage.

How About a Pomato for Lunch?

What plant looks like a vegetable, is treated like a vegetable, is eaten in 85 percent of all North American homes, but is actually a fruit? The tomato, of course.

Agriculturally, tomatoes are big business. In the United States alone, the tomato industry is worth nearly $4 billion each year. Yet, for all of its value, many people complain about the taste of the tomatoes that are sold in stores.

The problem is that tomatoes taste best when they are allowed to ripen on the vine. But tomatoes that are allowed to ripen on the vine tend to rot too quickly. Shoppers who like to eat tomatoes all during the year often find either rotten tomatoes or tomatoes that are hard and tasteless. Biotechnology is changing all that.

Over time, a tomato naturally begins to soften and spoiling sets in. Like many other functions, this one is caused by a specific gene. Several years ago, scientists identified and located the gene responsible for rotting. One company in California developed a way to remove the gene from the tomato, reverse it, then return it to the tomato. This process slows rotting by nearly 90 percent. The company has marketed the genetically altered tomato, calling it FlavrSavr. This product can now ripen on the vine, be harvested, then shipped to stores where it will remain fresh and tasty on grocery shelves three times longer than other tomatoes. The FlavrSavr is being gobbled up by consumers who love to eat tomato sandwiches all during the year.

Another company, DNA Plant Technology Corporation, has also developed a genetically engineered tomato that stays ripe on the vine for two months. Once it's picked, this tomato, called VineSweet, remains fresh on store shelves or in homes for nearly four months.

AMAZING FACTS

Your mother is right after all. Fruits and vegetables really are necessary for your good health. Researchers have found that nutritional deficiencies in an organism can cause a virus to mutate, becoming deadly.

Using mice that had been genetically-changed, scientists discovered that a human virus not normally harmful to mice, changed in malnourished animals. The mutated virus then was able to damage heart muscles in the mice. Once the virus mutated, it was also able to enter and infect healthy mice.

The ability of malnutrition to make a virus more harmful shows how important good nutrition really is. If a person suffers from poor nutrition, can he or she become more easily infected by viruses such as those causing meningitis or hepatitis? An unhealthy diet may make it easier for diseases to infect us.

Specially developed dwarf fruit trees have been genetically engineered to make harvesting easier. Fruit species can be engineered for several reasons — to produce more blossoms, to be pest resistant, and to make the fruit last longer.

Scientists have even taken the DNA from a tomato and fused it to the DNA of a potato, producing a pomato, or a tomato-potato hybrid. Can you imagine what the pomato tastes like? Next time you're in the grocery store, why not look for these products on the shelves?

Fat-Free French Fries?

Tomatoes aren't the only fruit or vegetable being genetically altered. As we process fruits and vegetables, we often prepare them in ways that allow for the absorption of animal fats, the most harmful kind of fats. Today, as families become more educated about the dangers of fatty foods, scientists are rushing to develop plants that resist the absorption of oil or fat.

Using genetic engineering, Monsanto Corporation, for example, has developed a high-starch potato. This new product reduces the rate of absorption of oil so it can be used to make french fries and potato chips that have less fat and fewer calories than the varieties of potatoes generally produced by modern growers

The Environment May Benefit as Well

Altering genes has other benefits, too. There has been great concern about the effects of pesticides on our environment. These chemicals (used for insect control) interfered with the development of birds' eggshells. The problem was so widespread that some species, such as the peregrine falcon, were placed on the endangered species list because scientists were afraid they were headed toward extinction. Pesticides were also found to kill fish and poison honeybees. They were found in unhealthy amounts in meat products, and they polluted our streams and rivers.

As researchers develop crops that are genetically resistant to disease and insects, we may also enjoy a cleaner environment.

This Nicotiana *plant is transgenic — genes from a soil bacterium, seen in the culture dish in the scientist's left hand, have been transplanted into it. In this way, resistance to herbicides, insects, and viruses can be introduced into a plant.*

According to the researchers, such products will not require the use of as many pesticides or fertilizers to grow successfully.

Will Natural Products Be History?

Already, there are over six hundred biotechnology companies involved in genetically engineering our everyday food products. Someday, in your lifetime, everything you eat may have been genetically altered in some way. Milk, fruits, vegetables, and animal products may all be improved through biotechnology in the future. Scientists will know how to multiply the "good" genes, destroy the "bad" genes, and transfer the most desirable characteristics from one organism to another.

Have We Learned from Past Mistakes?

In the past, our ecosystem sustained itself through natural selection. The strongest characteristics of living organism survived, while weaker ones did not. Over time, this process usually made organisms stronger. But biotechnology replaces natural selection with artificial choices.

Based on our past experiences, it's easy to see why some people are concerned about the decisions we sometimes make. History is filled with examples of researchers' mistakes. Even transferring a whole animal from one ecosystem to another can have disastrous results. Consider what happened with the starling and the gypsy moth.

In 1890, one hundred starlings, birds common to Europe, were brought to the United States and released in New York City. Because they were not native to North America, the birds had no natural predators. They multiplied and spread rapidly. Today, starlings can be found throughout the country, particularly in the north and mid-Atlantic states. They are so plentiful that, in many places, they are considered a public nuisance and pose a health threat to people.

AMASING FACTS

In March 1995, scientists produced fruit flies with large, complete eyes grown all over their bodies, including on their legs, wings, and antennae. The researchers hope they have found the "master control gene" that controls the development of the eye. Until now, scientists had not been able to identify those mechanisms that control how specialized body parts are formed. If they have discovered it, they hope to unlock the secret of exactly how cell differentiation takes place.

Can the embryo of an extinct animal be implanted in another live animal and develop normally? This is yet another possibility being considered by researchers.

In 1977, an entire baby woolly mammoth was discovered preserved in ice. Scientists have taken DNA samples from the animal and analyzed them. If at some point, they perfect a method by which an embryo can be formed from the frozen tissue, then perhaps a bison, an elephant, or a musk ox can be used as a surrogate parent, allowing the embryo to develop into a live baby mammoth. Similar experiments are also being considered using tissues taken from other animals found frozen in time. This might also provide a way for researchers to save endangered species.

The baby woolly mammoth that was found in Siberia, Russia, in 1977. Scientists may one day be able to develop a live baby mammoth from the frozen tissue of this relic of the Ice Age.

Like the starling, the gypsy moth originally came from Europe. In the mid-1860s, a naturalist brought the moth to New England, hoping to breed it for silk production. But some of the caterpillars escaped from their enclosures and invaded nearby fruit orchards.

Both hardy and very destructive, the moth spread rapidly. Today, the moth has been found as far west as Oregon and as far southwest as Arkansas.

The ecological problems created by scientists experimenting with the starling and the gypsy moth still have not been solved. That's why, when scientists began experimenting with genetic transfer, many people became concerned about possible effects on our ecosystem. Scientists do not always fully understand the impact of their experiments. What if entirely new, deadly organisms were developed? It is possible that researchers still may create something that could cause long-term problems or even a disaster. That is why they must continue to conduct their research using the strictest control methods.

Chapter 5
The Shape of Genes to Come

A plasmid is a length of DNA, occuring in bacteria and yeast, that can exist outside a chromosome and replicate itself. Foreign DNA can be spliced on to plasmids and then introduced into different bacteria. Plasmid genes have useful properties such as resistance to antibiotics and the ability to produce toxins that may keep away insects.

Throughout history, animals have been important to us. Historians believe that the first wild animals were domesticated thousands of years ago. Even in recent times, a person's wealth was often determined by the amount of livestock he owned. So it's no surprise that animal biotechnology is booming.

At about the same time that Watson and Crick were identifying the structure of DNA, other scientists discovered that DNA material is found not only in chromosomes within the nucleus of the cell but also in other parts of the cell. This proved to be an exciting discovery! Free-floating DNA material is much easier to capture and retrieve — and thus to use in genetic engineering — than the material locked inside the cell nucleus.

The other tools needed for genetic engineering are the proteins that cause chemical reactions in cells. Researchers can use these proteins, called enzymes, like scissors and paste, cutting DNA into segments, then gluing the segments onto other DNA molecules.

With a supply of available DNA material and enzymes that could be used to "snip" it into segments, scientists could transfer genes from one organism to another. This process of mixing a DNA segment from one organism with

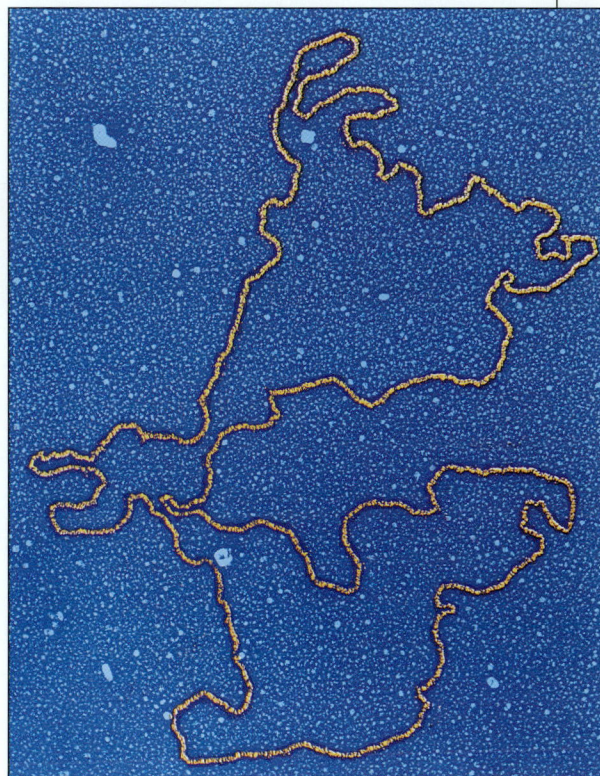

This African violet contains a transposon, or jumping gene — a mobile piece of DNA that can move about through an organism's DNA and make changes to it, depending on where it is positioned. A transposon has caused this plant to sprout a single purple flower among the pink ones.

DNA from another organism results in an organism that has an entirely new genetic structure, known as *recombinant DNA.* Any offspring produced by the restructured organism also has the new DNA structure.

From the Lab to the Table

One of the goals of genetic scientists is to alter livestock in a way that will produce greater amounts of food to feed the world's population. One of the most successful products of this science is the genetically engineered dairy cow. Bovine somatotropin (BST) is a genetically engineered growth hormone that is injected into dairy cows. The use of BST can increase milk production by 30 percent, but it has also caused controversy. Some people argue that the United States does not need to increase its dairy production. Also, there is concern because BST causes diarrhea and bloating in cows. Farmers then treat the cows with antibiotics. Small amounts of those antibiotics show up in the cows' milk, posing a possible hazard to people allergic to those antibiotics. And because genetically altered products do not have to be labeled as such, shoppers may not even realize they are buying milk that has been changed in such a way.

The Food and Drug Administration (FDA), a federal agency that monitors food production, does not require labeling of altered foods because the agency does not believe there are any major differences between the new foods and the old natural products. But others are not so sure that we know or understand how the new artificial foods may affect our long-term health. These are some of the problems faced by researchers and consumers as we begin to use genetically altered products.

Mighty Mice

In 1980, the first transgenic mice — which carry genes from another species or breed of animal — were bred. Other mighty mice soon followed. Mice give scientists the opportunity to study the effects of different diseases and to test the ability of genetic engineering to treat those diseases. At The Ohio State University, scientists have developed mice whose genes now include a rabbit growth gene. These altered mice are more than twice their normal size. Can the same research be applied to cattle? Scientists believe it may be.

Experimental mice are infected with viruses treated to implant human genetic disorders into the animals. Gene therapy can then be tested and developed on mice rather than on humans.

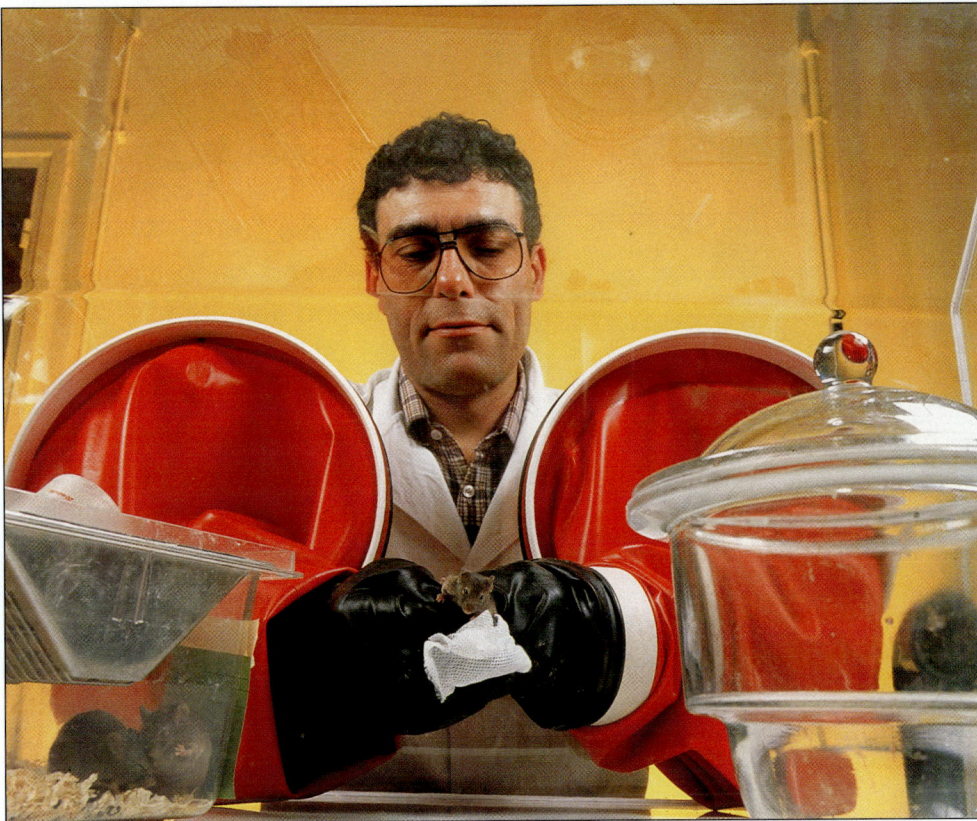

43

Mary-Claire King

One of the most significant discoveries in the field of genetics was made by a graduate student just twenty years ago. Mary-Claire King shocked the scientific community when she concluded that 99 percent of human DNA is exactly the same as the DNA of a chimpanzee. Her research supports the conclusion that man and chimpanzee have evolved from similar, if not the same, lineages.

King was born in 1946 in Wilmette, Illinois. Her father, Harvey King was an executive for an oil company; her mother, Clarice King, was a homemaker. Mary-Claire remained in the Midwest throughout her childhood and pursued her undergraduate degree at Carlton College in Minnesota. Three years later, she graduated with honors and enrolled in a doctoral program at the University of California.

King was interested in the University of California because, in addition to its strong graduate program, it also had a reputation for political activism. As soon as King arrived on campus, she began protesting against the Vietnam War and other government activities. In 1969, she even took a leave of absence from school to accept a research fellowship at Ralph Nader's Center for the Study of Responsive Law. While there, she worked on a project that evaluated the effects of pesticides on migrant workers.

In her graduate program, King began working with Dr. Allan Wilson, studying the differences between man and chimps. She became increasingly frustrated because she was unable to find any differences between the two sets of samples. Even though she was frustrated, King's results were

spectacular. Her research demonstrated just how similar the gene pools for the two species are.

Since that discovery in 1975, King has focused her research on the hereditary causes of breast cancer. According to the latest forecasts, one in eight women in the United States will develop breast cancer. Her most recent studies conclude that between 5 percent and 10 percent of all breast cancers can be traced to a single dominant gene. In 1990, King, working with a team of researchers, located the gene responsible for early-onset familial breast cancer on chromosome seventeen.

King has a personal stake in her research. Both her sister and sister-in-law have had the disease, and she is also at-risk for it. In addition to her research, King serves on the Special Commission on Breast Cancer of the President's Cancer Panel, as well as on numerous advisory panels, task forces, and commissions. Since the late 1980s, King has also focused on the AIDS epidemic among homosexual men, and she is studying an inherited type of deafness that affects families, especially in Latin America.

Yet despite her heavy workload, King provides assistance in the use of genetic information to find missing persons. She has worked in Argentina for families seeking lost children, and she has assisted the United States Army in identifying the remains of soldiers recovered after the Vietnam War.

In 1992, King perfected a technique in which DNA is taken from teeth and then compared to other specimens in hopes of finding a match. The procedure can be used when a body has decomposed to the point that the only remains are skeletal and no dental records exist. Law enforcement officials believe the procedure will be valuable in helping to solve cases that have remained unsolved for years.

King is also heavily involved in the Human Genome Project. She has lobbied for continued funding for the project and continues to search for common bonds between all humans.

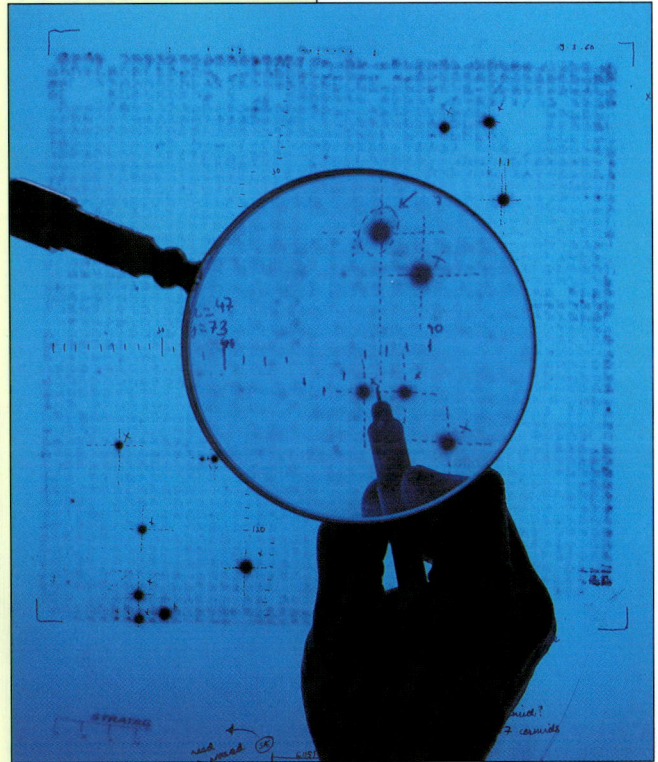

DNA fragments on human chromosome seventeen are studied in an attempt to find the defective gene responsible for many cases of inherited breast cancer.

Another strain of mice has been developed that may be able to carry the gene responsible for sickle cell anemia. This sickness, which mainly strikes black people, interferes with the blood's ability to carry oxygen. It results in painful swelling of the hands and feet and enlargement of the heart. Researchers believe the experimental mice may be used to help them find a cure for this disease.

Can Researchers Own Living Organisms?

But can live organisms like these be patented? That was the question Ananda Chakrabarty wanted answered. Remember the oil-eating microbes that were used to help clean up the oil from the *Exxon Valdez* spill? In 1972, Chakrabarty was a young researcher who worked for General Electric Company. Chakrabarty had developed a strain of bacteria that was capable of breaking down four types of fuel.

The scientist decided he wanted to patent (be given legal rights to) his bacteria, so no one else could use his organism

As well as creating bacteria that break down fuel, Ananda Chakrabarty has created a bacterium to feed on the chemical Agent Orange, a defoliant widely used in the Vietnam War, which causes diseases and birth defects in humans.

These transgenic lambs were born to ewes that have had a human gene incorporated into their DNA. The gene is resonsible for the production of the protein alpha-1-antitrypsin (AAT). This protein can be isolated from the sheep's milk and used to treat AAT deficiency in humans, a hereditary condition that leads to emphysema, a lung disease affecting about 100,000 people worldwide.

without his permission or payment to him. No one had ever before patented a living organism. The case went to the U.S. Court of Customs and Patent Appeal. The court agreed with Chakrabarty. The judges said that even living organisms can be patented if they have been developed through human research.

In 1992, the U.S. Patent and Trademark Office agreed to patent three kinds of "mighty mice." There are now over two hundred additional applications for transgenic animals. Patents allow a scientist to own an animal developed through genetic transfer. Researchers believe that this should be done so that their discoveries will be protected. But many people disagree.

Some people believe that patents take away the rights of animals. Others object to patents because they treat live creatures as products that can be bought and sold.

So far, no other country has agreed to patent living creatures. In 1992, the European Parliament recommended against such patents. But the concern about patents and animal welfare will continue. In fact, as more genetically-altered animals are produced, the question is likely to become more complex. And we will continue to struggle with it for years to come.

Chapter 6
Solving Genetic Puzzles

When Alexandra, the empress of Russia, gave birth to a son in 1904, she and her husband, Emperor Nicholas, already had four daughters. Unfortunately, Alexandra was the granddaughter of Queen Victoria of England. Queen Victoria had been a carrier of hemophilia, a genetic disorder passed from one generation to the next through the X, or female, chromosome. Nicholas and Alexandra first realized something was terribly

Britain's Queen Victoria (lower center) poses with several generations of her family at Coburg, Germany, in 1894. As a carrier of hemophilia, she passed on the gene responsible to her daughters, but the disease itself only appeared in some of her male descendants.

wrong when soon after birth, Alexis bled uncontrollably from his navel. The disease was not confirmed until Alexis was two years old, but once Nicholas and Alexandra knew for certain that Alexis was a hemophiliac, they had to hide his condition from everyone. They knew that if people found out about it, Alexis would never be allowed to become emperor of Russia.

So young Alexis was forced to lead a sheltered life, kept from any activity that might cause him to cut or bruise himself. Hemophilia ruled every moment of his life.

The Human Side of Genetic Engineering

In general, there are three groups of genetic diseases. First, as suggested by Thomas Hunt Morgan and his fruit flies, there are *sex-linked* abnormalities. In most cases, such diseases are X-linked, that is, the female chromosome carries the abnormality. Because females have two X chromosomes and the trait is recessive, a female will not get the disease unless both of her X chromosomes carry it. A male, on the other hand, who has only a single X chromosome, may inherit the disease if he receives the recessive gene from his mother because he has no healthy chromosome to dominate the recessive one.

Hemophilia is a prime example of this type of disease. When Queen Victoria of Great Britain became a carrier of hemophilia, she passed the disease on not only to the Russian emperor's family but also to the Spanish royal family. Females carry the gene, but male heirs are the ones who suffer from it.

A second class of genetic diseases are *autosomal recessive*. Typically, in autosomal recessive diseases, the healthy gene is dominant, thereby preventing the onset of the disease.

Perhaps the most famous autosomal recessive disease is cystic fibrosis. Although 5 percent of the population carry the cystic fibrosis gene, only one in every sixteen hundred individuals acquires the disease. Cystic fibrosis is a complex disease to study because it causes such a variety of symptoms and also because it is fatal. Patients suffer from breathing difficulty, tissue infections, and the accumulation of mucus in the lungs and pancreas. Few live to adulthood.

It was only fifty years ago that cystic fibrosis (CF) was first identified. Today, about twelve million Americans (mostly Caucasian) carry the defective gene. Scientists around the world searched for the cause of the disease. Lap-Chee Tsui found it.

Tsui was born in 1950. He arrived in the United States at the age of twenty-four in order to pursue graduate studies at the University of Pittsburgh. Eventually, Tsui moved on to conduct research at Toronto's Hospital for Sick Children in Canada. As part of his research, Tsui studied fifty-four families who carried the disease. From that study, he concluded that the culprit gene was located on chromosome seven. That was the easy part.

Working via telephone, facsimile messages, and the mail, Lap-Chee Tsui and Francis Collins had to locate the hidden gene between two genetic markers that were 1.6 million bases apart. It took them four years to find it.

Their collaboration opened the floodgates for locating specific genes. And now that the responsible gene has been identified and located, there is increasing hope that a cure for cystic fibrosis will soon be found.

The third class of genetically-inherited diseases is *autosomal dominant*. In this group, all those who carry the disease are also infected with it.

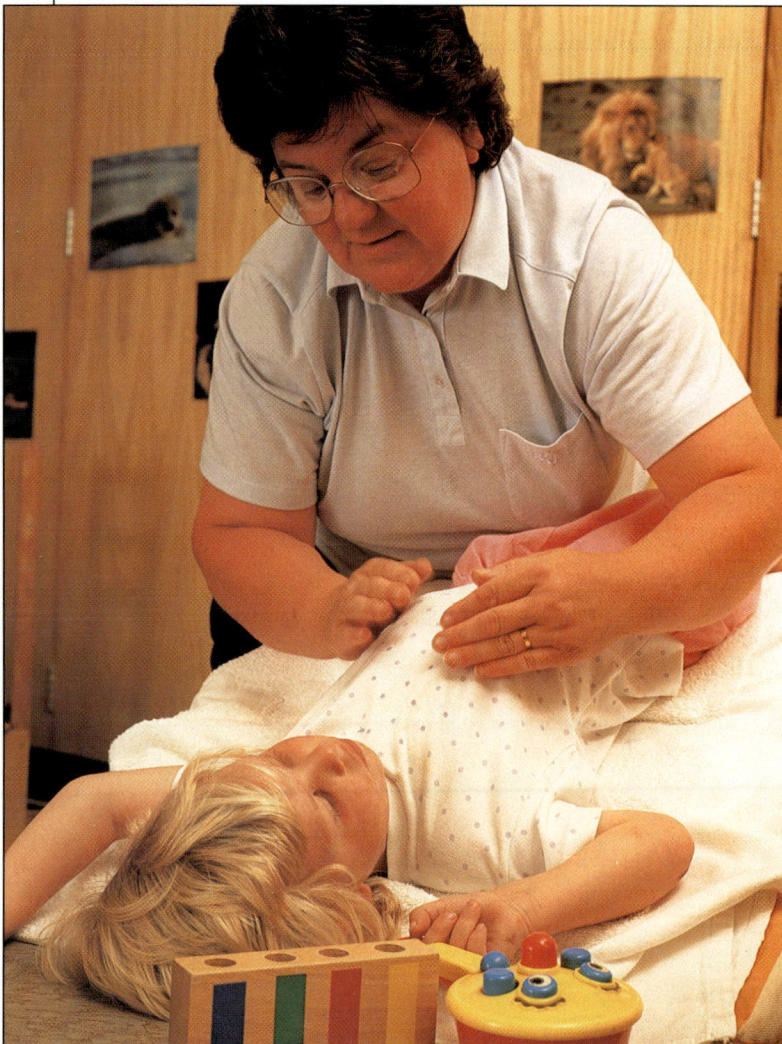

A physiotherapist helps a three-year-old cystic fibrosis patient breathe by loosening the thick mucus in the child's lungs. Now that scientists have located the gene that causes CF, it is more likely that a cure for the disease will eventually be found.

Huntington's chorea is just one of the autosomal dominant diseases. While it doesn't strike until a person is an adult, it seriously affects the nervous system. But usually by the time a patient is diagnosed with the disease, he or she has already passed it on to offspring.

In all, there are approximately four thousand inherited diseases. Researchers have pinpointed the general location of many of them. Thus, it is only a matter of time before their exact locations are found.

Producing Proteins

Genetic engineering has also helped us produce large quantities of the proteins we need to treat diseases. There are two kinds of such proteins.

The first are those proteins that may be deficient in humans, thereby causing diseases like diabetes, which is caused by a lack of insulin, the hormone that regulates blood sugar levels. By using genetic engineering to produce vast amounts of proteins, like insulin, medical specialists can readily replace the proteins missing in affected patients.

In the past, insulin was available only through the pancreas of a pig or a cow. Now that it can be produced through genetic engineering, it is safer, less expensive, and more readily available to patients everywhere.

The second kind of protein, a *biological response modifier*, controls body functions. There are very small amounts of these proteins available in the body, but we all need them. Endorphins, for example, are proteins that act as natural painkillers. If these proteins can be produced for commercial use, they may be cheaper and safer to use than other treatments.

Researchers are also learning to control disease by taking certain human cells, such as blood cells, treating them, then returning them to the body. This process, called *somatic cell gene therapy*, may successfully treat diseases caused by mutant genes.

AMAZING FACTS

Once in a while, the rules of genetics don't seem to apply. Are there occurrences that "break the rules," or is it just that we don't know all the rules yet?

Scientists know that the AIDS virus spreads its genetic message from one individual to another through body fluids such as blood. Thus, if a woman is infected with the HIV virus, there is a strong possibility she will pass the disease on to her unborn child. Then, the child will remain HIV positive throughout his or her life. Or at least that's what normally happens.

But a boy from Los Angeles who contracted the disease from his mother has startled researchers. Typically, children born HIV positive develop AIDS sometime during their first three years. Instead, this youngster lost all symptoms of the disease. Although he is tested at regular intervals, he remains disease-free. Doctors don't know if the virus is still there, but his health has remained excellent. He may have actually beaten the disease.

Francis Sellers Collins

Perhaps no one in the world today is associated more closely with biotechnology than Francis S. Collins. His scientific discoveries continue to amaze the research community.

Francis S. Collins, the youngest of four boys, was born in Staunton, Virginia, to parents who valued education, the arts, and the discovery method of learning. Collins' father had a Ph.D. in English and taught at a nearby college, while his mother was a playwright. So highly did his parents regard learning, they chose to teach their sons at home rather than sending them to public schools. Thus, from the time he was just a toddler until he completed fifth grade, Collins was home-schooled by his mother.

Collins began attending school in the sixth grade. While he was in high school, he discovered his love for chemistry, and he pursued it through high school and through his undergraduate education at the University of Virginia.

While he was at Yale University working on his graduate degree, Collins became fascinated by genetics and the study of molecular biology. He graduated from Yale in 1974, earning both his M.S. and Ph.D. degrees. He then entered the University of North Carolina School of Medicine where he began his serious interest in genetics and graduated as an M.D. in 1977.

After three years of further study at Yale, Collins became an assistant professor of genetics at the University of Michigan. It was there that he perfected the technique of chromosome jumping (*see* Chapter 3). This enabled him to help locate the gene that causes cystic fibrosis. In addition, Collins has also located the gene that carries neurofibromatosis.

Medical research is an extremely competitive field. Quite often, a number of scientists are working to unravel the same mystery, and there is often a race to see who will be credited with a particular discovery. In this competitive environment, Collins stands out. He is extremely well-liked by fellow scientists and regards himself as a "team player."

In addition to his own religious upbringing, Collins was greatly influenced by the writings of C. S. Lewis. He has developed strong religious convictions and makes no apologies for them.

Francis Collins (center) celebrates the discovery of the gene that causes cystic fibrosis. With him are fellow scientists Lap-Chee Tsui (left) and Jack Riordan and a little girl who suffers from the disease.

Rather, Collins has translated his beliefs into action. In 1989, for example, he traveled to Nigeria, volunteering for several weeks at a missionary hospital.

Collins is also motivated in his research by a sincere compassion for patients who suffer from the diseases for which he is trying to find cures. These feelings help drive him in his scientific endeavors.

In 1993, Collins was appointed as the director of the Human Genome Project at the National Institutes of Health. In that capacity, he is responsible for coordinating the research, hiring scientists, and providing overall direction to the effort.

While some investigators may be driven by the desire for power or fame, Collins seems to be guided by a natural ability to solve the mysteries of genetics. That may be why he has been so successful in his discoveries. At times, he finds what he is looking for long after other scientists have given up.

Human Reproduction Will Never Be the Same

A human egg is examined to see if it is suitable for fertilization. In the in-vitro fertilization process, fertility drugs are given to a potential mother to stimulate the production of several eggs. These are then harvested and fertilized. If fertilization is successful, several embryos are returned to the woman's uterus in the hope that one will implant.

Not only has genetic science changed the way we approach inherited diseases, it has also permanently altered the human reproduction process. Artificial insemination, for example, lets a woman's egg be fertilized through a safe medical procedure. Women who have a difficult time becoming pregnant may also be treated with fertility drugs. These drugs chemically stimulate the ovaries to release an egg. The major side effect is that use of the drugs sometimes results in multiple births.

Since 1978, in-vitro fertilization (IVF) has also become increasingly popular. This process allows a female egg to be fertilized in the laboratory, then returned to the uterus for development.

IVF was developed in Britain by physiologist Robert Edwards and gynecologist Patrick Steptoe. First used in 1978, the process was considered both experimental and controversial; many people argued that it carried science one step too far.

In-vitro fertilization quickly became an accepted practice in the medical community. There are now numerous clinics around the world that promote the technique. Today, one hundred thousand children have been conceived through the in-vitro technique.

Unusual stories have come to light about babies born through the in-vitro technique. In Britain, for example, genetically twin brothers were born two years apart. After the eggs had been fertilized, one was immediately implanted in the mother. The other was stored to be used at a later date. Eventually, both fertilized eggs produced the twins.

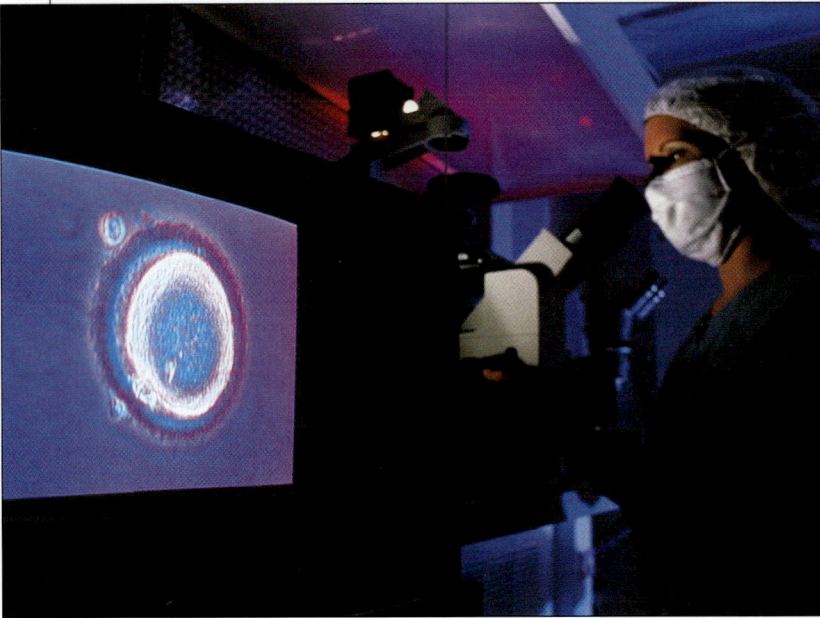

In South Africa, a woman was implanted with fertilized eggs belonging to her daughter and son-in-law. Because her daughter was unable to carry the fetuses to term, the mother volunteered. The pregnancy was successful, producing a set of triplets. While the woman is genetically the grandmother of the babies, she was legally listed as their mother.

What are the problems with in-vitro fertilization? One major question is what to do with the unused, fertilized embryos. Sometimes they are frozen until the parents decide what to do with them. But what happens if the parents die or divorce? As more parents use biotechnology to assist them with childbirth, these questions will have to be answered.

Whose Property Is It?

One of the most controversial aspects of genetic engineering is the question of ownership. If a researcher removes a tissue from a patient and uses it to produce a medical product, then who owns the product, the researcher or the patient? If the new product saves lives, can the owner of it decide who will be treated and who will not? It is estimated that humans have between fifty thousand and one hundred thousand different types of genes. If even a fraction of them are used to produce new medical products, who will own them and how will they be used? As the field of genetic engineering grows, questions such as these will face researchers, patients, courts, and society.

Although these two boys were conceived on the same day, they were born a year and a half apart. Thanks to IVF treatment, twelve eggs were produced from the mother and fertilized by the father. Half the embryos were implanted in the mother's uterus at the time, while the others were frozen and used eighteen months later.

Chapter 7
The Human Genome

Doctors now believe that, for the first time, they have successfully used gene therapy to treat a disease at birth. In 1993, three children were born suffering from severe combined immunodeficiency, or the "Bubble Boy" disease. The disease is caused by an absence of the gene that manufactures the adenosine deaminase enzyme, known as ADA. Usually children with "Bubble Boy" disease become infected and die before reaching the age of one, so they must live in a sterile environment to prevent any infections. The common name for the deficiency comes from a boy known as David who lived in a sterile environment, a large plastic bubble, for twelve years before dying in 1984.

Immediately after the children's births in 1993, medical specialists took blood from the babies' umbilical cords and added a normal ADA gene. The treated cells were then reinserted into the children through blood transfusions.

In order to help the babies fight infection, doctors have continued to give them shots of ADA. Now that the children are toddlers, however, researchers believe the gene therapy has worked. They are reducing the amount of ADA given to the children in hopes that, over the next few months, their bodies will begin to manufacture their own immune cells.

The Biggest Human Library

The far-reaching implications of gene therapy led scientists to believe that every gene in the human body should be identified and located. In 1986, a group of American scientists suggested

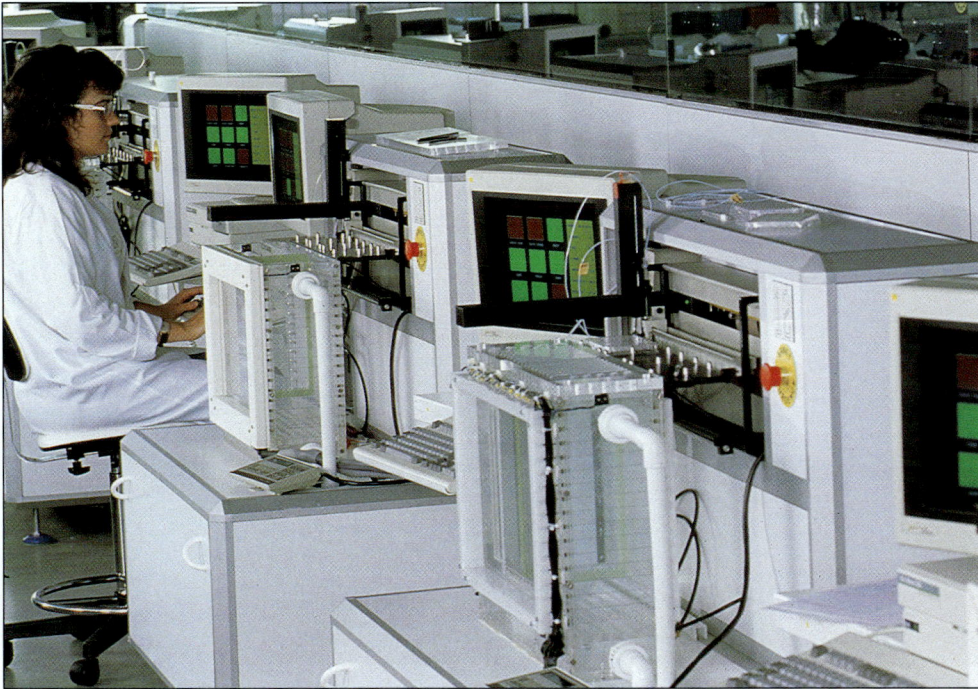

Human genome research involves sorting and deciphering vast amounts of DNA, a tedious and time-consuming task. Here, the Human Genome Project uses automated electrophoresis equipment to speed up the process. Patterns and sequences of DNA are displayed and analyzed on computers.

that a project be undertaken to map the entire human genome, the complete set of human genes.

Once the Human Genome Project was proposed, a National Research Council Committee was formed to study the issue. In 1988, after a year-long study, the committee recommended that the Human Genome Project be an international effort. When the project officially began in October 1990, the United States, Great Britain, France, the European Community, and Japan all participated. Additionally, genome projects were also begun in Canada, Italy, Russia, the Netherlands, and Scandinavia. Together, all the international programs, involving over five thousand scientists, are coordinated through HUGO, the Human Genome Organization. HUGO promotes the sharing of ideas and information.

When the project was first proposed, it was anticipated that it would cost approximately $1.00 to locate each base pair and that it would take fifteen years to map all of them. That meant that the effort would cost three billion dollars and would not be completed until the twenty-first century.

AMAZING FACTS

The Human Genome, or library of all human DNA material, is thought to hold some "junk reading" as well as critical genetic blueprints. In fact, researchers believe that only about 5 percent of human DNA makes up the genetic library. Most of the base pairs of chemicals are "filler" DNA that has no specific function necessary to human development.

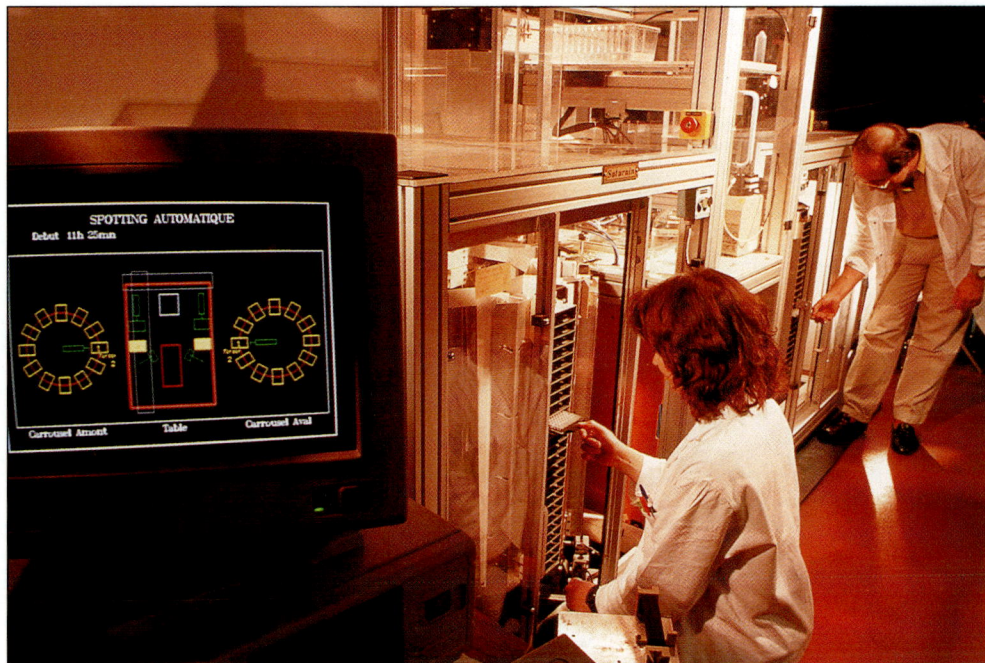

Large quantities of DNA are stored in the Human Genome Project. In this automated gene library, the equipment handles giant artificial yeast chromosomes that store large amounts of DNA in one chunk.

Reaching Out

James D. Watson, the Nobel prizewinner who, with Francis Crick, had first described the double helix structure of DNA, became the first director of the Human Genome Project. In April 1993, Dr. Francis S. Collins replaced him as the director of the project. At that time, the mapping of genes was ahead of schedule, so Dr. Collins has chosen to focus more on diseases caused by genetic mutations.

Dr. Collins also wants scientists to share more information so they can more quickly understand, diagnose, and treat or prevent diseases. And as part of the project, scientists want to study more families that suffer from inherited diseases. Such studies can provide critical data gathered over time from multiple generations and can help medical specialists learn to track inherited illnesses better.

Finally, the Human Genome Project may help scientists understand how combinations of abnormal genes or interaction between genes and the environment cause disease. Many cancers and mental illnesses, for example, are believed to be brought on by a combination of inherited and environmental factors.

Long-Term Effects

Top researchers predict that just ten years from now we will be able to use a simple blood test to get a complete genetic history of an individual. But the moral issues raised won't be that simple. Can such information be used to discriminate against those with abnormal genes? How much information about a person's genetic makeup can be kept confidential? Should genetic profiles be provided to educational institutions, employers, or insurance companies, or could that information be used against an individual in some way?

Everyone agrees that the Human Genome Project and the advances being made in biotechnology raise medical, legal, social and ethical problems. There are few easy answers. As the science of biotechnology evolves, these questions will have to be addressed. But most researchers believe that the long-term gains far outweigh the risks. Biotechnology holds the promise of helping us live longer, healthier lives.

There is no turning back. The wave of biotechnology has overtaken us. It is impossible to guess what the future might hold for us. What we do know is that biotechnology can give us answers to questions that have haunted us for generations — questions about diseases and abnormalities, questions about our food supplies and our environment, and questions about how long and how well we will live. The challenge facing all of us is to use biotechnology only for the good of human beings and to fight any attempts to use it for any other reason.

A new technique to determine the distance between genes and a way of ordering them along a chromosome is under development. An enlarged cell nucleus is projected onto a screen to allow measurement with a ruler. DNA probes containing yellow fluorescent dye are attached to specific parts of the genome. The distance between the yellow points relates to the number of base pairs between the probes.

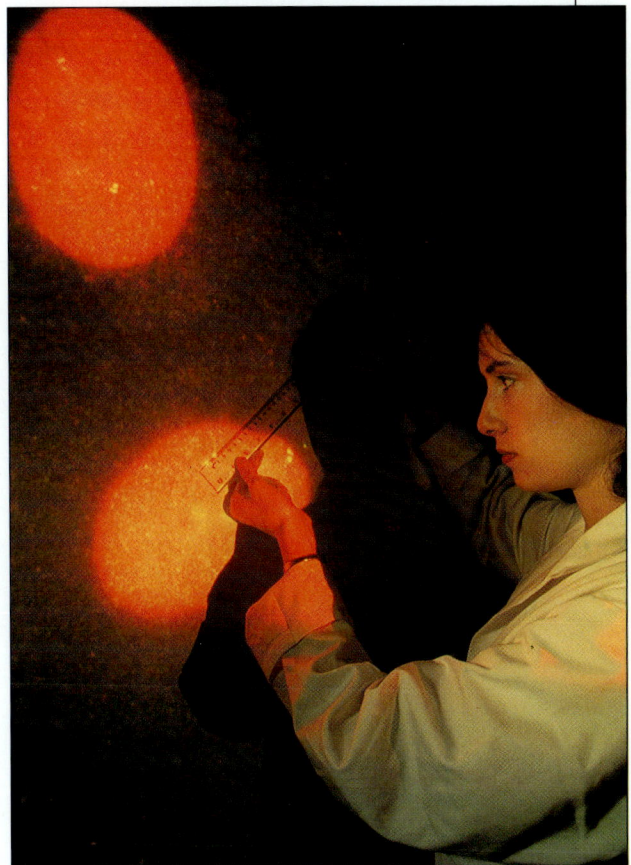

Timeline

1866 — Gregor Mendel describes patterns of genetic inheritance.

1868 — Johan Friedrich Miescher discovers presence of nuclein (nucleic acid).

1906 — William Bateson coins the word "genetics."

1915 — Thomas Hunt Morgan discovers that certain hereditary traits are sex-linked.

1944 — Oswald Avery, Colin MacLeod, and Maclyn McCarty discover that genes are comprised of deoxyribonucleic acid (DNA).

1949— Scientists prove that a mutant recessive gene is responsible for sickle cell anemia.

1953 — James Watson and Francis Crick discover the double helix structure of DNA.

1961 — The first part of the genetic code is broken by Marshall Nirenberg and Johann Matthaei.

1970 — Hamilton Smith and Daniel Nathans perfect a method of using enzymes as scissors to snip strands of DNA.

1973 — The first gene is cloned.

1978 — The first child, Louise Joy Brown, is born using in-vitro fertilization.

1980 — U.S. Supreme Court rules that an oil-eating bacterium can be patented.

1988 — The Human Genome Project is approved. Researchers locate the gene responsible for Duchenne muscular dystrophy.

1989 — Lap-Chee Tsui and Francis Collins locate gene responsible for cystic fibrosis (CF).

1995 — First cases of children successfully treated for severe immune deficiency disease using gene therapy.

Further Reading

Aronson, Billy. *They Came From DNA*. New York: W. H. Freeman and Company, 1993.

Asimov, Isaac. *How Did We Find Out About DNA?* New York: Walker and Company, 1985.

Asimov, Isaac. *How Did We Find Out About Genes?* New York: Walker and Company, 1983.

Backwill, Fran. *DNA Is Here to Stay*. Minneapolis, MN: Carolrhoda, 1993.

Bornstein, Sandy. *What Makes You What You Are: A First Look at Genetics*. New York: Julian Messner, 1989.

Fichter, George S. *Cells*. New York: Franklin Watts, 1986.

Gamlin, Linda. *Evolution*. London: Dorling Kindersley, 1993.

LeMaster, Leslie Jean. *Cells and Tissues*. Chicago: Children's Press, 1985.

Nardo, Don. *Oil Spills*. San Diego: Lucent Books, 1990.

Glossary

Chromosome: A rod-shaped chain located in the cell nucleus that carries the genetic information for the cell. It is made up of DNA, RNA, and protein.

Clone: An exact copy of another organism with exactly the same genes.

DNA: Deoxyribonucleic acid. A double helix-shaped chemical structure (similar to a spiral staircase) that holds all the genetic instructions for an organism.

Enzyme: A natural protein that brings about chemical reactions in cells. Researchers have learned to use some enzymes like scissors to cut segments of DNA.

Gene: A segment of DNA that acts as identifying codes for hereditary traits. A type of miniblueprint for an organism.

Genetic engineering: Methods and techniques used by scientists to change the genes located within cells of living organisms.

Genetics: The study of heredity.

Genome: The full set of all genes in any organism.

Heredity: The function by which traits or characteristics are passed from one generation (parents) to the next (offspring).

In-vitro: Refers to procedure conducted in an artificial environment outside the living body.

Mutation: A natural, random change in a gene that results in an altered organism. May be accelerated by radiation, temperature changes, or chemical reactions.

Nucleic acid: The substance within the nucleus of a cell that includes DNA.

Nucleotide: The basic building block of a DNA (or RNA) molecule.

Recombinant DNA: DNA material from two or more different organisms that has been joined together.

RNA: Ribonucleic acid. The nucleic acid involved in translating DNA into proteins.

Transgenics: The process of inserting DNA from one organism into another host organism.

Index

Numbers in *italic* indicate pictures; numbers in **bold** indicate biographies